FIVE RUSSIAN STORIES

FIVE RUSSIAN STORIES

An introduction to contemporary Russian literature with
introduction, commentary and notes

**ARNA BRONSTEIN
ALEKSANDRA FLESZAR**

UNIVERSITY OF NEW HAMPSHIRE

A FOCUS RUSSIAN READER

ISBN 1-58510-058-7

Book Team:
Publisher: *Ron Pullins*
Editorial Manager: *Cynthia Zawalich*
Production Editor: *Allison Roger*

Printed in the United States of America

10 9 8 7 6 5 4 3 2 1

CONTENTS

ACKNOWLEDGMENTS

We would like to thank Mikhail Dymarsky for his invaluable aid in obtaining the stories from each author and for researching and clarifying many cultural references. His work was instrumental in the completion of this reader. We are indebted to all of the authors whose works appear in this reader, and we feel fortunate to be instrumental in bringing their work to an English-speaking audience. We would also like to thank Jason Merrill for his comments and suggestions that added much to this work. A special thanks goes to Ron Pullins of Focus Publishing for his support and publication of this project; his help in bringing works of contemporary Russian writers to an English-speaking audience is instrumental in facilitating an understand of another literature and culture.

MIKHAIL DYMARSKY

ABOUT MYSELF

I was born in Leningrad in 1957, exactly 15 years after Paul McCartney. My father is a mathematician, my mother is an engineer. I am half Jewish, one quarter Belorussian, one quarter French; my upbringing and soul, without a doubt, are Russian. After finishing school in 1975 I enrolled in Leningrad Hertzen State Pedogogical Institute (now called the Russian Hertzen State Pedogogical University), in the department of Russian language and literature. I graduated in 1979, then served in the army from 1979-80 (stationed about 10 kilometers to the south of Arkhangelsk.) After this I worked as a teacher of Russian language and literature in an elementary school; but from 1981 I also taught part-time at the Hertzen Institute. (I taught contemporary Russian language.) In 1986 I entered graduate school in the same institute in the Department of Russian Language, and in 1989 I defended my Candidate's dissertation [the first higher degree in Russia, the equivalent of an American ABD].[1] I also worked there - as a senior lecturer in the department. From 1996-99 I was in the doctoral program, in November 1999 I defended my doctoral dissertation; now I am a Doctor of Philological Sciences [PhD]. (I still cannot get used to this idea.) In 1992, together with some friends, I founded a Russian-American journal of Russian philology *Russkij Tekst* [Russian Text], and I was chosen as its main editor. Six issues have been published.

I play the piano and guitar, and in my spare time I have written a few songs based on the poems of Russian poets. I love jazz (especially traditional and avant-garde), the Beatles, Pink Floyd, Deep Purple... I like folk songs and songs written by my friends. I also love my family and my

---

[1] ABD – All But Dissertation. This is a designation given to those who have completed all the coursework and exams for a PhD degree, but who have yet to complete a dissertation.

mother. My wife, Elena, teaches mathematics in a high school. I have three children; my oldest (Anna) lives in America, Katya is a university student, and Dima is in high school.

INTRODUCTION

The authors whose works are included in this reader are writing today; they are writing during a period when Russian literature and its artists are "finding themselves" in the post-Soviet period of rebuilding and redefining a nation, Russia, and its political, economic, social and artistic endeavors. The writers represented in this reader, although living in this new era, were educated during Soviet times and were raised on works of Socialist Realism, the artistic doctrine of the Soviet Union. In order to study their works in light of the current changes, it is beneficial to understand what Soviet literature aimed to present to its readers and how Russian literature, while moving away from Socialist Realism, has changed in the last several decades. A review of the historical background can provide insight into where the current literary endeavors may be heading.

Socialist Realism, an artistic doctrine that was defined by Andrej Zhdanov in his speech at the first All-Union Congress of Soviet Writers in 1934, outlined the aesthetical program of the former Soviet Union. Zhdanov prescribed that the writer must "know life in order to know how to depict it truthfully in artistic works, to depict it not scholastically, not inanimately, not simply as 'objective reality,' but to depict reality in its revolutionary development."[1] He further states that "the truthfulness and historical concreteness of the artistic portrayal should be combined with the problems of ideological remolding and the education of the toiling masses in the spirit of socialism."[2] Thus, during the Soviet period the writer was expected to depict life truthfully and to combine this realism with socialist ideological content.[3]

---

[1] Speech of the secretary of the Central Committee of the All-Union Communist Party A. A. Zhdanov, *First All-Union Congress of Soviet Writers 1934 Stenographic Summary* (Moscow: Artistic Literature, 1934), p. 4.

[2] *Ibid*, p. 4

[3] For further reading on socialist realism, see E. J. Brown, *Russian Literature since the Revolution* (New York: Collier Books, 1969); Katerina Clark, *The Soviet Novel: History as Ritual* (Chicago: University of Chicago Press, 1981); Geoffrey Hosking, *Beyond Socialist Realism: Soviet Fiction*

One of the central characteristics of this artistic method was that of realism as defined by its proponents. An artist was supposed to present reality; however, he/she reshaped it according to the ideological principles of socialism. This remolding of reality was accomplished in accordance with the necessary socialist beliefs of the writer or the pretense of these beliefs. Guided by this ideology the writer was required to choose his/her topic from the surrounding reality.

If an artistic work was to "remold and educate," it had to be accessible to the people.

As Lenin stated, since "art belongs to the people.... It should be understood and loved by the masses."[4] Thus, art assumed a political role. As a socialist, it was expected that one's sympathies lay with the working masses, and therefore a true socialist writer aimed to serve the interests of the masses.

Socialist realist art looked forward into the future, finding the beginnings of the future in the present reality. Inherent in the doctrine was the desire to make history, to portray reality optimistically. There were subjects that were forbidden and subjects that were obligatory. Since authors had to actively support the building of the socialist state, socialist realist art could not lack ideology; it had to condemn the bourgeois system (with its emphasis on the individual) while praising socialism, its construction and its future goals (accomplished by the workers.)

Socialist realism was not, however, a static doctrine, but rather one which changed with time and was adapted by theorists, political leaders, critics and artists themselves as the situation in the country and events dictated. During the 1930s and 1940s the doctrine was adhered to strictly, thus prohibiting any experimentation or straying from the most important message of socialist realism: the portrayal of "reality in its revolutionary development" and the "education of the masses in the spirit of socialism." Some early examples of socialist realist literature include *Cement* by Fyodor Gladkov (1924-25), which is considered by many scholars to be a precursor to socialist realist works, *Time, Forward!* Valentin Kataev (1932), *How the Steel was Tempered*, by Nikolai Ostrovskii (1934) and *Young Guard* by Aleksandr Fadeev (1945.) The plots of these novels revolve around a hero (or collective of heroes) who are faced with a task (which supports the socialist state either to build it in the face of destruction after the Revolution and

---

since "Ivan Denisovich" (New York: Holmes & Meier, 1980); J. C. Vaughn, *Soviet Socialist Realism: Origin and Theory* (New York: St. Martin's Press,1973).

[4]   "Lenin about the Art of a New World: Excerpts from the book *On Literature and Art*," in Mikhail Parkhomenko and Aleksandr Miasnikov, *Socialist Realism in Literature and Art* (Moscow: Progress Publishers, 1971), p. 28.

Civil War or which supports the Soviet Union against the fascist enemies of World War II.)

The 1950s, with the death of Stalin, and the leadership of Krushchev, brought about a "thaw" in the arts, some loosening of restrictions on the arts, while still retaining the doctrine of socialist realism in principle and in function. There were, however, complaints that Soviet literature did not reflect true reality, that the fate of the individual in the Soviet state was not presented in literary works. During this "thaw" writers began to portray a more true reality, not only the reality as proscribed by the tenets of socialist realism. Changes did not take place immediately, and there was much discussion among writers and literary theorists and critics. By the time of the 2nd Congress of Soviet Writers in December 1954 these issues had not yet been resolved. In February 1956 Krushchev denounced Stalin at the famous 20th Congress of the Communist Party, and there was a further relaxation of many restrictions until November of that year when the Hungarian revolt took place, and many restrictions were once again implemented. During this brief thaw works which adhered to the doctrine of socialist realism were published (Vladimir Dudintsev's *Not by Bread Alone*, 1956) as well as works which were critical of Stalin's USSR, such as Aleksandr Solzhenitsyn's work *One Day in the Life of Ivan Denisovich* 1962.

The death of Stalin did allow for debates and for different factions (conservatives and liberals) to discuss the arts. Finally a policy of some tolerance emerged, and individual experiences began to appear as themes in Soviet literature. This struggle between liberals and conservatives continued during the 1960s; some writers strongly demanded artistic freedom while others criticized the questioning of the Party's authority in the arts.

Works officially published during the 1960s included some experimentation in themes and ideas, while speaking more openly on contemporary issues. Writers were looking to find freedom in the artistic process, freedom in their choice of themes and freedom in writing styles. However, the vast majority of artistic works published still adhered to the Party's restrictions on the arts.

By the 1970s the adherence to the tenets of socialist realism was weakening, but there did not emerge a new soviet artistic theory or a reworking of the restrictions of socialist realism. While earlier writers wrote under the restrictions of socialist realism, in the 1970s there was a period of discussion and debates during which the literary theorists and critics tried to adapt socialist realism to works that were actually already written, and therefore give socialist realism a "human face." Theory was reacting to practice. Editors were cautious, hampering "the evolution of real talent by avoiding originality, changing style and using a number of other means to emasculate the main idea of a work of art and remove the individual-ity of the writer from the work he has created."[5] N. N. Shneidman, who has written extensively about the changes in Soviet/Russian literature in the 1970s-1980s, characterized the literature of the 1970's as literature of affirmation: "It is supposed to affirm the Soviet way of life and to justify the policies of the Communist party and the Soviet government."[6] Literary works could not be anti-soviet, nor could they reject the Communist Party and Soviet principles.

The 1980s brought a new freedom to the arts and a more open discus-sion of social and political issues, although there was still no tolerance for open challenging of the Soviet Union and its policies. Shneidman explains, "[t]he development of Soviet literature is a process in which socialist realism evolved from being a realistic method of presentation, in which the reflec-tion of reality was 'typical,' to an ideological and emotional affirmation of certain phenomena and the expression of a certain world-view."[7] What remained most important was the adherence to *partiinost'*, party principles and spirit.

The role of Soviet literature, first and foremost, had been an edu-cational one, designed to present an ideology that would influence the people. While the range of permissible themes widened, this educational role remained. When Gorbachev became leader of the Soviet Union in 1985, many works of literature, which had previously been censored, were published, although there remained some limitations, and censor-ship still existed. Literary debates continued, but the politics of the Soviet state persisted in influencing writers. Gorbachev believed that past evils should be discussed before future achievements could be realized; he felt there was a need to change the mentality of the Soviet people to be morally and socially responsible, and literature was to be an important vehicle in making these changes.[8]

With the collapse of the Soviet Union, the rise of Russia and the sub-sequent disappearance of controls or censorship, the arts have exploded in many directions, while writers have begun to examine and discuss previously taboo subjects, including pornography, past evils of the soviet system, and current social and economic crises within the country. It is in this broad field of literary topics and styles that one finds the authors

---

[5] N.N. Shneidman, *Soviet Literature of the 1970s: Artistic Diversity and Ideological Conformity* (Buffalo: University of Toronto Press, 1979), p. xii.

[6] *Ibid.*, p. 13.

[7] *Ibid.*, p. 11.

[8] *Ibid.*, pp 30-31.

presented in this reader. Although these writers were educated under the Soviet system (or during the collapse of it), their range of topics and styles has not been limited by Soviet censorship. They are enjoying the artistic freedom that now prevails, and their choice of topics, vocabulary and styles reflects that freedom.

The themes explored in this collection range from adultery and true love, to science fiction, to criminality and the question of the hero, to the questioning of religious beliefs, and to the disappearance of an old way of life in modern day Siberia. These works were chosen to represent some prevailing trends in contemporary Russian prose, to introduce the reader to a small, but representative, sample of what is happening in the literary world of Russia today. It will remain to be seen if these trends will continue or be replaced by entirely new ones.

When choosing the stories, we found that in these stories the underlying theme was the search, by each author, for something that had been missing in the Soviet Union. As George Gibian, in his introduction "The Quest for Russian National Identity in Soviet Culture Today," in the work *The Search for Self-Definition in Russian Literature*, states, "One major theme in Soviet Russian cultural life today is the question: What has happened to the Russians? To their society, their land, water, air? What will and what should happen to Russia?"[9] Although Gibian is discussing Soviet literature, the same questions and searching are evident in Russian literary works during and after the fall of the Soviet Union in 1991. Glasnost literature of the 1980s asked the questions "Who is to Blame?" "What is to be Done?"; a quest for answers based on the titles, respectively, of Herzen's work and Chernyshevsky's work of the 19th century. Majorie Balzer explains this surge of consciousness as "… an inner searching for lost cultural values and traditions."[10] This search has led some contemporary writers, such as those included here, to a re-examination of old Russian and Soviet values, of Russian and Soviet morality and emotions.

This search for answers is continuing today as writers examine the social and intellectual development of literature. We have included Mikhail Dymarsky's commentary on each of the stories because his views can be used as a mirror into the contemporary intellectual conscience in Russia today. His analyses provide insight into how a Russian literary scholar may

---

[9] George Gibian, "The Quest for Russian National Identity in Soviet Culture Today," in Ewa M. Thompson, *The Search for Self-Definition in Russian Literature* (Texas: Rice University Press, 1991), p. 2.

[10] Majorie Mandelstam Balzer (ed.) *Russian Traditional Culture: Religion, Gender and Customary Law* (New York: M. E. Sharpe, 1992), p. ix.

look at contemporary Russian literature. Dymarsky is a Doctor of Philological Sciences, teaches courses on Russian literature in St. Petersburg and is editor of a Russian-American journal of Russian philology *Russkij Tekst*. (see his autobiography on p. viii)

The first story, Igor Mezhuev's "A Strange Event" asks the questions: What is reality? What is the fantastic? As Valery Popov's story "Dreams from the Top Berth"[11] asked what was real in Soviet society, Mezhuev asks what is real in Russian society today. In Popov's story the main character, while riding on a train, encounters, what may seem to be fantastic occurrences, such as the conductor's keeping chickens in the bathroom, and a restaurant car on the train which serves goulash, a meat stew, which has no meat. Mezhuev's story describes the "flight" to Mars; there is a question as to whether this flight has ever taken place, and no answer is ever provided. Is reality the same for all?

Vladimir Monakhov's hero in "A Defrocked Monk" is searching for religion; having left the monastery, he is still deeply religious, quoting from the Bible and blessing a dead infant, but he is also trying to find his place in the world. After over seventy years of socialist atheism, the Russian people are once again turning to religion and searching for religion's place in modern Russia and in their individual lives. Is religion the same for all?

Ilona Yakimova, in her work "Romance with a Sequel," is one of many women writers today, and there is much discussion (both in the West and in Russia) as to whether there is a woman's voice in Russian literature today. Is there a "woman's voice" or are there simply women authors? Are there "woman's themes" in Russian literature or themes that women authors more often address? Yakimova's search centers on the role of art in a woman artist's life. Is art the same for all?

Mikhail Butov examines the place in modern Russia for a by-gone era when one could live on the unspoiled land of vast Siberia, as does his hero in "Relict." The environment and the damage inflicted upon it in the name of socialist development are being debated and discussed in Russia today as citizens and government are exploring ways of how to deal with the necessary clean-up of environmental disasters which are a legacy of Soviet industrialization. In addition, the "nationality question" has long plagued the Soviet Union and Russia; the advent of glasnost in the 1980s brought this question into the open as citizens began to voice their opposition to russification. Is progress the same for all?

Vladimir Lavrishko's hero in "In the Thick Fog" is an anti-hero accord-

---

[11]   Found in Helena Goscilo and Byron Lindsey (ed.) *Glasnost: An Anthology of Russian Literature under Gorbachev* (Michigan: Ardis Publishers, 1990), 293-302.

ing to the principles of socialist realism. During Soviet times there existed a Soviet morality; a set of moral principles which guided behavior and actions. Today modern Russia is searching for a social morality: What is this morality based on? What is good? What is evil? The questions raised in this story center around the concept of what is the morality and what is a hero vis-à-vis social mores and morality. Is morality the same for all?

These stories were chosen for a varied audience: students of Russia, Russian history, political science and literature of all levels, and for those who are interested in Russian contemporary society and literature. The questions raised by these authors are ones that are being discussed in Russian today, and which, when examined, can provide some insight into contemporary Russia and Russian thought.

The format of the stories is as follows. Each story is one complete chapter that includes a cultural discussion of the story (in the context of contemporary Russian society and the theme of searching,) a short biography of the author, a translation of the story itself (with cultural footnotes), an analysis by Mikhail Dymarsky and a set of suggested questions/themes for either written or oral discussion.

A STRANGE EVENT

In Soviet times the version of reality presented in the arts was that which was prescribed by Socialist Realism, a reality "colored" by the socialist artistic doctrine and followed by writers who wished to be published by the Union of Soviet Writers, the only vehicle for publication in the USSR. The Union also controlled salaries and offered benefits such as dachas (country houses) and speaking tours "...dangl[ing] before the writer as positive inducements to follow the developing official traditions of the Soviet novel."[1] Thus, writers were bound by the tenets of socialist realism for their livelihood; if the government-owned publishing house did not publish the writers of an author, that author was not published in the Soviet Union, and thus not considered a writer. Since it was illegal not to work under the Soviet system (one was called a "parasite of the state" and subject to legal punishment), if a writer was not published in the Soviet Union, he/she had to find other gainful employment.

Following the doctrine of socialist realism, a writer had to portray reality "in its revolutionary development." The reality of socialist realism (see Introduction, p. i) was not the true reality surrounding the writer and society, but a reality overshadowed by the building of socialism, thus a reality as the government "wanted it to be." This reality was often seen as illogical and irrational. One need only look at Valery Popov's story "Dreams from the Top Berth" (originally published in the journal *Iunost*, December, 1987) to see an illustration in prose of the "absence of reason in the circumstances of everyday Soviet life: the conditions under which the protagonist takes what should have been a rather mundane train ride pile one irrational absurdity upon another in a topsy-turvy world that ultimately makes minimal human comfort the pinnacle of one's dreams."[2] The absurdities which

---

[1] Katerina Clark, *the Soviet Novel: History as Ritual* (Chicago: The University of Chicago Press, 1981), p. 4.

[2] Helena Goscilo & Byron Lindsey (ed.), *Glasnost: An Anthology of Russian Literature under Gorbachev* (Ann Arbor: Ardis Publishers, 1990), p. xxxviii.

are confronted in the story are abundant. The protagonist has obtained a train ticket *nalevo* (that is "to the left", outside the system), and proceeds to describe the strange trip in which the male conductor of the car is dressed in woman's clothing, there is no heat (the story takes place in the winter) in the train car and no coal to heat the water for tea, the conductor is keeping chickens in the bathroom, the restaurant car only serves cold goulash (a meat stew from which the waiters have stolen the meat); the list of absurdities continues. At the conclusion of the story (after the waiters have been arrested for theft and after the protagonist worries what the chickens will think of him when he uses the bathroom, "Would they [the chickens] be insulted by the act I was planning to perform there?"[3]), the narrator realizes that he cannot complain about the problems on the train, since as he says, "… the matter of my questionable ticket might come up…"[4]

Alexandra George describes the period of Soviet rule as "… a Theatre of the Absurd in which appearance took the place of reality and nothing was what it seemed…"[5] Most recently Vassily Aksyonov, a writer and teacher who now lives and works in the United States, was quoted as saying, "reality is so absurd that by using the method of 'absurdization' and surrealism, the writer sort of tries to harmonize the disintegrating reality."[6] In Mezhuev's story "A Strange Event" the author presents an event which was not what it seemed; the reader is left to question if the event really took place: Did John Brighton ever land on Mars?. According to the narrator no one lost sight of the "rocket" (visual reality) and John insists he was on Mars, but there was an absence of John's pulse during the flight. Thus, the question of appearance and reality is questioned and distorted. The author has taken "reality", such as it is, and given the reader a seemingly realistic story in which the reality is questioned.

In addition to portraying a distortion of reality, Mezhuev plays upon the pattern of the tradition of the Russian *skazka* (fairytale), as outlined by Vladimir Propp in *Morphology of the Folktale* (1968) and discussed by Maria Kravchenko in *The World of the Russian Fairytale* (1987). According to Propp's model, the basic underlying structural element of a fairytale is a journey during which the hero is confronted with ordeals on his/her quest to return home. Mezhuev uses John Brighton, an unlikely hero, and his journey to an impossible place, Mars, as the central action of his short story. John Brighton is an anti-hero, a physically small man (who was chosen to travel to Mars because he fit into the "sarcophagus-can the size of a suitcase"), a man of enormous ideals ("a fighter for peace, a former

---

[3] Valery Popov, "Dreams from the Top Berth," as translated in Helena Goscilo & Byron Lindsey, p. 301.
[4] *Ibid.*, p. 295.
[5] Alexandra George, *Escape from "Ward Six": Russia Facing Past and Present* (New York: University Press of America Inc., 1998), p. 7.
[6] As quoted in Russian Life (July/August, 2002), p. 19.

naive Marxist") who is taking this journey to call attention to his words of love and peace for all peoples.

This story of a successful journey to Mars (or unsuccessful as it is unclear whether John Brighton ever left Earth) is also a story belonging to the genre of Soviet/Russian science fiction, a genre that although not widely known to those living outside of the Soviet Union, has existed and flourished. As Isaac Asimov states, "…if there was any doubt that the Soviet Union was science-fiction-oriented before Sputnik I went off like an alarm in the night, surely there was no doubt afterward."[7] Soviet/Russian science fiction is often "marked by humane feeling."[8] Although there were some works of science fiction that stress the action-type, American works of the genre, "the preoccupation of the authors remains with social problems, human values, high ideals."[9] Mezhuev's John Brighton is a shining example of a protagonist who believes in humane feelings and a higher ideal (that of international peace among different nationalities). Magidoff continues, "[the characters in the works]… in present-day Russian science fiction [1968] are presented first and foremost as dreamers with visions of universal happiness, soldiers in the service of peace, veritable 'Don Quixotes' of humanism."[10] This is, indeed, an accurate description of John Brighton.

Asimov also notes that often the action of Soviet science fiction takes place in the present or relatively near future. Mezhuev's work makes no reference to the time of the story, but it seems to the reader that the action has taken place only recently. Some cultural references (the birthday of the Queen, the parliamentary system of government in Great Britain, Castro's gift of a watch to John Brighton) suggest that the action is in the present time.

In conclusion, Mezhuev makes use of the genres of the Russian *skazka* and Russian science fiction for his own means: to create a present-day story which makes his hero an anti-hero in the style of the Russian *skazka* and to use elements of the humane atmosphere of Russian science fiction to make his hero a far greater one than his stature would suggest. Both the *skazka* and science fiction are an antithesis of the socialist realist genre, and Mezhuev's humorous referents to the achievements of Soviet society facilitate his antithetical position.

In reading this story one should also keep in mind that for the USSR, space exploration and "being the first to get there" was of utmost importance. Kosmonauts (astronauts) were heroes larger than life and their accomplishments were presented as great feats, reflecting on the greatness of the Communist Party and the Soviet Union. Is John Brighton such a hero?

---

[7] Isaac Asimov, *Soviet Science Fiction* (New York: Collier Books, 1962), p. 10.

[8] *Ibid.*, p. 13

[9] Robert Magidoff, *Russian Science Ficton 1968: An Anthology* (New York: New York University Press, 1968), pp vii-viii.

[10] *Ibid.*, p. viii.

IGOR MEZHUEV

ABOUT THE AUTHOR

Igor Mezhuev was born in 1962 in St. Petersburg. He graduated from Leningrad State University with a degree in physics, and for several years worked as a scientist in the area of Arctic and Antarctic exploration. Several times he spent the winter at the Soviet Polar station (in the Antarctic.) Since then he has spent extensive time in Canada and in Great Britain, has hitchedhiked around Europe and has been a teacher of English. He writes both prose and poetry and has been published in Russia, Poland, France and Germany. At present he is also employed as a computer programmer and lives in the town of Gatchina, a city in the Leningrd oblast 27 miles from St. Petersburg (Leningrad). Formerly a summer resort for that city, it has a population of about 90,000 and is known for its unique park and 18th-century palace.

A STRANGE EVENT

by Igor Mezhuev

1994, St. Petersburg, Russia

During my visit to the British Space Exploration Center, I happened to witness a strange event.

In honor of the International Year of Geophysics, America and Russia decided to send manned spaceships to Mars.

Our British colleagues had no intention of lagging behind the space superpowers, but since the new Tory cabinet provided a rather low level of funding for science programs, they were not in a position to build a multi-staged rocket. Their funding allowed only for a single-stage rocket with a hard body gunpowder engine. If I remember correctly, this rocket was approximately four feet long.

John Brighton, an old friend of mine, a fighter for peace, a former naive Marxist, famous for his unusually small stature and vivid speeches in Parliament supporting National Liberation movements in the farthest reaches of our planet, offered himself to the British Space Center as an astronaut. Since there were no other volunteers, and all the British societies for the prevention of cruelty to animals had, as a united front, come out against sending a dog or a guinea pig, the Space Center, without much deliberation, accepted Brighton's candidacy and forwarded the appropriate paperwork to the Upper House of Parliament for approval. Unbelievably both houses immediately and unanimously voted to send John into space.

I met John long before his flight to Mars. We met at a bus stop, in the drizzling rain. Fog, so treacherous for a simple London man without a car, enveloped the thorny mass of the Parliament building. I stood there pondering the future of space exploration, and in light of my thoughts Big Ben seemed to be a rocket aimed at the limitless breadth of cosmic space. Suddenly my attention was diverted to a boy who was standing there, munching on chips from a paper bag. He looked lost and defenseless. I came up to him from behind and tenderly hugged him, hoping to warm him up under the plaid lining of my Macintosh. He picked up his head and a pair of eyes, wise and tired from a long battle with the injustices of this world, the eyes of a grown man, stared back at me. I remember, precisely at that moment Big Ben struck midnight, and from his pocket John took out a red velvet rag with a watch in it; he looked at the watch and said:

"It's exactly three hours behind Moscow time."–he neatly wrapped the bundle back in the velvet cloth and explained–"It's a 'Polyot'[12] watch."

While we waited for the bus, we became true friends.

Of course the rocket could not fit even John's miniature body, and thus my British colleagues proposed a new and original variation on the manned flight. John was placed in a small sarcophagus-can the size of a suitcase. The sarcophagus consisted of several "cans" sort of floating inside each other in a thick oil-like substance. This original design was intended to soften the blow of landing on the surface of Mars or Earth.

The sarcophagus-can was tied to the rocket by a 15-inch inflammable Kilvar[13] thread. In case of an accurate landing on Mars, there was an unspoken agreement between the Russians and the Americans that they would deliver John and his sarcophagus back to Earth.

During the preparations for flight we often knocked gently on the sarcophagus to give John support during this moment that was so difficult for all of us, but particularly difficult for him.

On the day of the scheduled flight garlands of holiday lights were hung all around.

Right before lift-off John gave a brilliant speech about world peace. He said that he had dedicated his life to the struggle for mutual understanding among various nationalities; he spoke of the illusory nature of borders between nations and peoples. Of course when I say he spoke, I mean he knocked in Morse code against the inner walls of the can, but his knocking was so inspired that I could hear in it John's intonations so familiar and dear to my heart.

As it became clear later, John made this heroic voyage not for his own glory, but to have the opportunity to tell people of his love for them and to force them to listen to his words. Unfortunately the day of lift-off coincided with the Queen's birthday, which distracted the general British public and did not elicit the appropriate interest on the part of the press corps.

I attended the lift-off with Professor Green. My duties consisted of telemetric and visual control of the flight.

The starting signal was given, "Ignition to lift-off, lift-off!", the professor lit the Bickford (safety) fuse, and the rocket began a slow lift-off, then the thread stretched and took with it the can containing John.

It is difficult to express the joy that filled our souls in the first seconds

---

[12] Polyot is the name of an old watch factory on the outskirts of St. Petersburg. The word itself means "flight."

[13] Kilvar is a special metal fusion with an extremely low expansion factor.

of the flight; it is difficult to express our pride in the victory of human thought over the power of gravity.

Nevertheless, in spite of numerous calculations and preliminary tests, the can turned out to be just too heavy for the four foot rocket, and having lifted off to a height of seven or eight feet, the rocket skidded, leaned over and slowly floated down the street in the direction of Trafalgar Square. That which Professor Green feared most happened–the thread began to catch on the garlands and wires of the holiday lights.

I grabbed a stepladder from the lab and ran down the street after the rocket, trying to nudge the can up higher into space, but within a couple of minutes the engine, not having allowed the rocket to reach the second stage of cosmic speed, fell into the Edward Lutyens fountain,[14] and having spit out a small, nasty cloud of yellow smoke, it died. The rocket began a catastrophic descent, and ignoring the fact that I was wearing new pants, I jumped into the fountain and just managed to catch the can with John in it.

When the can was opened and an exhausted and worn out John stepped out of it, Professor Green apologized to him for the failed experiment. However, paying no attention to the Professor's apologies, John began to enthusiastically describe his first steps on Mars. The only thing that seemed to upset him, he said, was that he lost his engraved watch, the one given to him by the legendary leader Fidel Castro himself.

You should have seen our surprise when the next evening, American astronauts who had returned from Mars announced on TV that in one of the Martian canals they had found the engraved watch belonging to the British astronaut, John Brighton, who must, therefore, hold the title of the first man to step on this mysterious planet.

This was indeed strange, since during the entire flight Doctor Green never lost sight of the can with John in it. On the other hand, the last check of telemetric data (Channel A-4) pointed to an absence of the astronaut John Brighton's pulse between the fourth and sixth minutes of flight.

---

[14]   A reference to one of the two ornamental fountains designed by Sir Edwin Lutyens (1869-1944), located in the center of Trafalgar Square behind the Nelson Monument.

ANSWER THE FOLLOWING

1. Describe the hero, John Brighton, from the narrator's point of view.
2. Describe the narrator.
3. Describe the setting.
4. What, in your opinion, is the theme of the story?
5. What is irony? Does the author use irony in this story? If so, how?
6. How did the ending of the story impress you? Were you surprised?
7. What do you think that the author wanted to convey in this story?
8. Are there poetic elements in the story?
9. Are there any comic effects in the story? What role do they play?

DISCUSS THE FOLLOWING

1. Do you think that this story is universal?
2. What do you think of the title of the story? How does the title relate to the story itself?

COMMENTARY

PROFANING THE PROFANE

by Mikhail Dymarsky

That is how one can summarize the idea behind Igor Mezhuev's "A Strange Event." Or to say less pointedly "ironizing irony." Actually, everything in this entertaining story is irony. While the existence of the "British Space Exploration Center" may be possible, all else–the interplanetary rocket measuring "approximately four feet," the "sarcophagus-can" about the size of a suitcase and tied to the rocket with a thread, the launching of this rocket with the help of a Bickford fuse from a laboratory in the center of London, and the very flight of this rocket and its ignominious finish–all this is so far outside the realm of reality, so concocted and playful that it can only engender a tone of mockery.

This mockery is particularly apparent in that the author keeps to a truly serious style of narration–even using ironic overaccentuation of that which has just been stated. Indicative of this style is a section beginning with the phrase "On the day of the flight garlands of holiday lights were hung all around." This phrase, by fact of omission, can be interpreted as an announcement of the streets being adorned in honor of the lift-off with John Brighton on board. However, four sentences later it becomes clear that the "day of the lift-off coincided with the Queen's Birthday," and there is no doubt as to the reason for this holiday lighting. But the author is most serious, and it appears that he is not being ironic and that he is sorry for this coincidence, and that it distracted the general public's attention from this historical lift-off. Behind these politely streamlined diplomatic formulas one can see traces of a total absence of attention by the British society. In addition, the topic for these two paragraphs is one that it would be sinful to treat with irony–love of humanity and "mutual understanding among various nationalities." These are holy concepts. It appears that the author laughs at all of this, since his hero knocks his "brilliant speech" in Morse code on the internal wall of the can.

It is also worth noting that the narrative style could not be better suited to the mocking character of the story. Numerous stock phrases and clichés, which during the Soviet period[15] were used to describe momentous events, provide an ironic contrast to the "realistic" and playful parameters of that which is described–"as a united front came out against," "gave a brilliant speech," "accepted a candidacy," "battle with the injustices of this world," "support during this moment so difficult for all of us," "made this heroic voyage," "interest on the part of the press corps." It would be difficult to say which serves as the object of reduction and travesty and which becomes a means of juxtaposition. On the one hand grand words are used to describe trite subjects, which creates the effect of mocking the event, and on the other hand, it can be interpreted as profaning these very grand words and concepts.

A particularly fantastic effect is brought about by certain absolutely non-traditional narrative expressions, distant not only from newspaper clichés, but also from norms of standard literary Russian. For example the phrase "In case of an accurate landing on Mars..." would be more appropriate in a discussion of shooting at the planet, but not in reference to a landing.[16] Even more entertaining is the description when the narrator, having grabbed the step-ladder, runs down the street after the rocket and tries to "nudge the can higher into space," as if it already were in space, just not high enough.

However, the conclusion of the story refutes all the assumptions regarding the object of the author's irony. This may or may not be a joke, but two objective and independent sources confirm that, which our reason-

---

[15]   Clichés were commonly used in the formulaic style of socialist realism. These clichés were seen on posters, in large letters on rooftops, in the press and in artistic works of socialist realism.

[16]   This is a reference to the Russian verb *popast' v*, which refers to hitting a target. The expected form in this context would be *popast' na* which refers to getting to a place.

able narrator and his colleagues see as absolutely impossible. It turns out that John Brighton actually was on Mars, although witnesses claim that his flight did not reach higher than five feet. The narrator insists that "during the entire flight Doctor Green and I never lost sight of the can with John in it." But could John have really been in it if the telemetric data showed "an absence of the astronaut John Brighton's pulse between the fourth and sixth minute of flight."

The reader has been provided with details of the "rocket" construction and of the "flight" process and although John himself is a somewhat funny and somewhat strange "fighter for peace, a former naïve Marxist," he did somehow manage to get to Mars. How did this happen?

It is not important how it happened. What is important is that it did happen. This is what topples all the irony that precedes the finale. It is the irony itself that turns out to be the object of new irony. Igor Mezhuev mocks our destructive habit of making fun of everything, of our desire for concrete usefulness and exactness at the expense of that which is most important, the spiritual, the insurmountable (that which John Brighton lives for)–the insurmountable, but nevertheless existing and defying profanation. Because the spirit conquers.

DISCUSSION

1.   Dymarsky believes that the small, "toy-like" size of the described object is juxtaposed to the grandiose phrases and clichés.
—What is the "object" he refers to?
—What grandiose phrases and clichés is he referring to?
—Is there a juxtaposition that he refers to? If yes, what is the effect or result? Is this a mocking of the clichés or is it profaning of high style expressions?

A DEFROCKED MONK

INTRODUCTION TO THE STORY

Although Prince Vladimir, in 988, adopted Russian Orthodoxy (in Russian *pravoslavny*, right praising, right believing) as the official church in Russia, for some time Russian Orthodoxy existed side by side with earlier pagan beliefs. Before Vladimir's conversion the people believed in higher deities and domestic ones (house spirits called *domovye*, from the Russian word *dom*–house). Vladimir believed that there was a need for a single religion that would unify the Russian tribes. (This assumed role of religion as a unifying force was used by many tsars of Russia, as well as by the Soviet leader, Stalin, during World War II.)

It is said that Vladimir sent out emissaries who were to report back to him about different religions and practices. Many were rejected for various reasons (e.g. the forbidding of meat and alcohol consumption), but the emissary returning from Hagia Sophia Church in Byzantium reported that in the church one could not tell if it were on earth or heaven, and thus Orthodoxy was chosen.

When Orthodoxy came to ancient Rus', so did its religious art and architecture, and the need for a written alphabet so that religious works could be used to educate priests and convert the people. (The Cyrillic alphabet was designed by the Byzantine monks, Cyril and Methodius; it is based on the Greek cursive alphabet.) Thus, early Russian art and culture came into being from the church. Religion became a unifying force in Russian society, a guiding force as the clergy attempted to blend Orthodoxy and pagan traditions in order to appeal to the masses.

The Russian Orthodox Church, the Russian branch of the Eastern Orthodox faith, places great importance on traditions of the past, traditions that are conveyed to the people by means of the liturgy and icons (religious paintings on wood.) In addition, Russian Orthodoxy is community-based, not individual-based (as are many Western religions); Alexander George explains that Russian Orthodoxy "… emphasized the idea of duties and obligations towards the community rather than individual rights."[1] This emphasis on the community is also seen in the early village structure in Russia that was based on the traditional village commune (*obshchina*) which controlled the land and agriculture.

A close relationship between the tsars and the Orthodox Church developed as the tsars believed they were chosen by God, even if in this relationship the church was subordinate to the tsarist government. Peter the Great (1682-1725), the great westernizer and reformer of Russia, in one of his reforms subordinated the church to the state; the church became a department of the state. A result of this reform, according to Alexandra George, was that "Peter the Great's reforms separated the church from the mainstream of Russia's culture."[2] The arts and culture were secularized, under Peter, as they moved away from religious influence. However, the role of the church in the tsarist government was still important.

The tsarist policy (begun under Nicholas I 1825-1855) of Orthodoxy, Autocracy and Nationalism (which stressed the importance of the unquestioned autocratic tsarist rule with Orthodoxy and the emphasis on Russian nationalism) demonstrates this relationship. Michael Florinsky describes Nicholas' thought: "A firm believer in autocracy, Nicholas held that a monarch 'by the grace of God' (and he recognized no other source of monarchial power) should be both the fountain of law and the actual head of the administration."[3] Earlier tsars also held this belief, but Nicholas "gave it a peculiar twist by emphasizing the importance of the dynastic and religious factors, by stressing the element of duty and discipline, and by insisting on conformity with national tradition."[4] While the government controlled the church, and the church was isolated from politics, "[T]he official church upheld the legitimacy of the government's cultural and social politics within the Tsarist Empire."[5] The church did little to address the social problems and inequalities under the tsars; it became isolated and stagnant.

However, the church, although under the tsarist government, still strongly influenced society and culture, so much so that the Bolshevik government and Soviet leaders, fearing all other authority, tried to build a society free from religion. "The Bolsheviks had to destroy the national Church

---

[1]   Alexandra George, *Escape from "Ward Six": Russia Facing Past and Present*, (Maryland: University Press of America, Inc., 1998), p. 20.
[2]   *Ibid.*, p. 156.
[3]   Michael T. Florinsky, *Russia: A History and an Interpretation*, vol. 2 (New York: Macmillan Publishing Co., Inc., 1953), p. 754
[4]   *Ibid.*, p. 754.
[5]   Alexandra George, p. 156.

as the spiritual backbone of the country"[6] so as to be able to replace this with Marxist-Leninist ideology. The church, hoping to avoid persecution, proclaimed its loyalty to the Soviet regime; however, the church was almost completely destroyed, during the purges of the 1930s and thereafter. Only during World War II, when Stalin needed the complete support of the Soviet people to defeat Hitler's invading armies, did the church enjoy some support from the government in the form of the reopening of 22,000 churches, two religious academies, eight seminaries and some monasteries.[7]

This reprieve from persecution lasted until the early 1960s when churches, monasteries and seminaries were again closed, and religious activity severely restricted. However, as Alexandra George points out, "[T]he church itself imposed a monolithic faith; ...it was intolerant of dissenters and non-promoting of freedom."[8] It has been a rare occurrence that anyone from inside the church has spoken out against the persecution. Most inside the church deny that the church was compromised by the Soviet government; they insist that the message of the church remained the same. As the Metropolitan of Vologda and Veliky Ustiug, Father Maxmilian, told Alexandra George in the mid-1990s "The first task of the Church is to instill moral principles in people. I don't think the Church is guilty of any wrongdoing."[9]

So where did this leave the Russian Orthodox Church in Russian society in 1981 when the story "A Defrocked Monk" was written by Vladimir Konstantinovich Monakhov? During the period immediately prior to the *perestrojka* and *glasnost* era of Mikhail Gorbachev (and the subsequent downfall of the Soviet Union), the church had been experiencing a revival. According to Marjorie Balzer, "[H]owever traditional values are currently defined, they are based on Russian Orthodox roots."[10] However, most agree that if Russian Orthodoxy is to enjoy a true revival and exert a real influence in Russia today, it must reform. As Alexandra George states, "If the Russian Orthodox Church is to be any kind of progressive force in society, it must define its role."[11] The church needs to reexamine its role; "[I]t is hard to see how the Church can provide guidance given the absence of intellectual leadership."[12]

In Monakhov's story the monk has left the monastery. He states that

[6] *Ibid.*, p. 159.
[7] *Ibid.*, p. 160.
[8] *Ibid.*, p. 21.
[9] *Ibid.*, p. 187-188.
[10] Marjorie Mandelstam Balzer (ed.) *Russian Traditional Culture: Religion, Gender, and Customary Law* (New York: M. E. Sharpe, 1992), p. x.
[11] Alexandra George, p. 157.
[12] *Ibid.*, p. 155.

he no longer believes in God, and that he was plagued by many questions for which the Bible and the monastic leaders could not provide answers. However, when he comes upon parents' grieving for their dead infant child, he gives them comfort by assuring them that the child is with God. It is clear that he has not rejected God. Perhaps he has rejected the out-of-date, traditional stance of the church which demands humility and asceticism, which expects its followers to accept the rituals without an understanding of their meaning, which has not drastically reformed or changed since its adoption in Russia over 2,000 years ago. The Russian Orthodox Church, the "right-believing" "right-praising" has not provided the answers for this defrocked monk; can it provide answers to the new Russian society?

VLADIMIR KONSTANTINOVICH MONAKHOV
THE AUTHOR ABOUT HIMSELF

I, Vladimir Konstantinovich Monakhov, was born 9 May 1947. I have been already known to the world for 53 years. I grew up in Gatchina. I am a professional artist. In 1965 I graduated from the Leningrad Art-Graphic Pedagogical School. After school I was a soldier; I worked drilling soil, taught children painting, drawing and modeling. I worked as a stage-painter. I restored monuments of wooden architecture. While doing all these things I also painted.

I began to exhibit in 1979. My works have been acquired by many art collectors in St. Petersburg and abroad. In art I adhere to the principle "All the world is mine." This is where my apparent absence of a clearly pronounced artistic image comes from. But this is what has given me the opportunity to build my own artistic world with all its variations.

Literature has fascinated me since the age of 10. I write short stories, poems, and commentaries on current affairs. And so literature and art have been going hand in hand in my life.

Since 1971 my works have been exhibited, with those of my colleagues, in St. Petersburg, Gatchina and abroad. However, during the past several years I have preferred to exhibit my works personally to an audience. My especially memorable Petersburg exhibits have been:

1990 Mayakovsky Library
1992 House of Scientific-technical Propoganda, Nevskij Prospect, 58
1996 Museum-Apartment of Dostoevsky

A permanent showing sponsored by the exhibit center "Viktronia" is in the lobby of the Gatchina film theater "Victory." I have had five open-air shows in Gatchina, a city in which I have lived and worked my entire life. Literature has been a fascination of mine since my youth.

A DEFROCKED MONK

by Vladimir Monakhov

1981, GATCHINA, RUSSIA

A marvelous day in the early part of the summer. A mirage from the heat of the earth hangs over the field. A barely perceptible wind brings the light aromas of different grasses. Long strands of clouds have become immobile way up in the sky, pouring out the warbling of sky larks. Everything is glowing with light.

A man walks briskly in the field along a barely perceptible path, and his black figure visibly stands out. Long dark hair sprinkled with gray. Bushy eyebrows. His trimmed beard, although not too short, is also speckled with gray. His long black frock is belted with a thin belt. The traveler is barefoot and has a bundle swung over his shoulder. He walks, looking often from side to side, and sings psalms, his voice mellow and rich. Judging by his appearance he is a monk.

– You are mistaken, my pompous clerk.[13] I used to be a monk, but I left the order. Now I am just a man. Andrew is my name.

– But you sing psalms.

– I don't know any other songs. I only sang this kind in the monastery. And I feel like singing. Look, what joy! And I'm even happier about the fact that I'm free.

– Then why are you wearing a cassock?

– Well, why a cassock, you ask? So far I've had nothing to change into. The monk in me died... two days ago. I left the monastery and still, somehow, I kept the faith. But when I walked along people's paths, it dried up once and for all.

– Did you really leave God?

– I him or he me, but I no longer believe in him. In the course of these days divine revelation descended upon me,–Andrew smiled–I clearly came

---

[13] pompous clerk – In this context this phrase is used ironically. The "defrocked monk" uses the most common and simple-spoken title of a simple man. "Pompous" (velerechivy) is an old and bookish adjective which stresses the irony. This irony stems from the fact that a secular man is trying to discuss biblical problems with a monk.

to understand that he does not exist. I'm thankful to him for that. For the first time in many years of serving him, I'm thankful to him, to God. You know, I was given to the monastery as an infant. For a long time I was a novice, and only then I entered the order. I studied the Gospel diligently, but the Old Testament even more diligently. Evenings in the monastery are long, and all you can do is sit and study the Holy Scripture. Father Superior regarded me with favor; I read with great studiousness. How else can you treat the Bible? But as the years passed, questions began to haunt me. I saw that not all is well in this world. Not everything attests to the truths of the Bible. I began to notice that our monastic leaders are not totally righteous. I saw many different people. There are the rich and there are the poor. Why is this so? I saw the stars in the sky, I saw the rotation of the sun – one in the summer and another in the winter. I saw civil wars where orthodox believers on both sides perished. I wondered at man himself, what is he made of, where is his soul? More and more often I looked in the Bible in search of answers.

– That's right, for the Bible is the treasure-house of divine revelations and human wisdom.

– I also thought so at first. But let us recall from the Bible the words of Jesus Sirakhov: " Do not test that which is out of your reach... Do not concern yourself with mysteries."[14]

I want to know, and Sirakhov from the Bible forbids it. And Solomon also instructs me in the same way: "Depend on God with your whole heart and don't depend on your own reason." Or "The beginning of wisdom is God's fear!"[15]

It would seem so: sit with your own questions and be quiet. But there are other words–words–those of Ezdra[16] "Truth is great, and it is greater than all."

These words suit me better. Does it not seem strange to you that such contradictions exist in the same Holy Book? You have no answer? But to me it seems strange. This is probably the reason why such deliberations on how the world was made are just empty talk. God made it so, and that is that. He couldn't have taken everything into account. He planned ahead how many

---

[14] Sirakhov–This reference is not found in either an English language nor in some Russian language editions of the Bible; however, there is a passage with this reference in the complete Russian edition, from The Book of Wisdom, ch. 3, v. 21. "Throughout the world do not seek the difficult for you, and do not strive higher than your strengths." Andrew paraphrases this verse.

[15] Proverbs, ch 3, v. 5

[16] Ezdra — This book is not included in an English language version of the *Bible*, nor is it found in some Russian language editions. It is included in the complete Russian language edition.

living and how many non-living things there should be in the world. Which creatures and how many of them. How many rich people and how many poor. How the poor should live and suffer. And then, you see, they will be rewarded in Paradise. That's the way it is in the Gospel. Riches are from God and poverty is from God. People need God to overcome their burdens. And burdens flow onto the poor in an unending stream. How many of them drop their hands in the hope of a bright life after death? They become like cattle. Paradise! But doesn't Ecclesiastes say in the Bible: "For everyone the same fate: the same for the righteous as for the sinner?"[17]

I hate all that is connected with God for he keeps me in darkness. I feel shackled by the chains of his teachings, his interdictions, his empty promises. Ecclesiastes was right when he said: "Do all that your hands are capable of doing, for when you die and go where you will go, there will be no work there, no thinking, no knowledge, no wisdom."[18]

Andrew became silent, took a breath and continued:

— And for what did Job suffer? You see, God decided to prove to Satan that Job's faith was true by making him suffer. But, he, Job, was a man, and not a scarecrow.

Andrew waved his hand and became totally silent.

— And where are you going?

— Where am I going? I asked for a leave from the monastery to visit the Kievan Cave Monastery,[19] to pray to the holy relics.[20] But at that time I wasn't sure that I'd make it there. Walking alone along these roads I was finally able to gather my thoughts, and I understood that I am free. I have finally thrown off the burden of worshiping a nonexistent idol. Now I'm going to see life. I want a full life.

And having again looked around, he walked on. A free man walks with ease!

The path began to go up along a gentle slope. Andrew quickened his path, wanting to see what's beyond the hill, what unknown places await. From the top of the hill a wondrous panorama unfolded. A huge wild field framed by a blue forest. Hills crowned with festive cumulus clouds, barely visible through the thick air, stretched beyond the forest. Andrew stood

---

[17] Ecclesiastes ch. 9, v. 2

[18] Ecclesiastes ch 9, v. 10

[19] Kievian Cave Monastery– a monastery founded in Kiev in 1051, located over caves where the preserved bodies of many monks lie

[20] holy relics–refers to the preserved bodies of monks lying in the caves of the Kievian Cave Monastery. The monastery is considered to be one of the oldest centers of Russian Orthodoxy, and the preserved bodies are thought to be holy. Ironically, during the Soviet period the government hung a banner on the gates of this monastery proclaiming religion to be the opiate of the masses (as stated by Karl Marx.)

enraptured. Isn't this a miracle! It makes you want to live! And just on this spot he cussed:

– Devils in cassocks.[21]

A large village was spread at the edge of the forest. The path led to this village. The closer it got to the houses, the more trodden it became. Other smaller paths flowed into it like streams. And here, the path itself flowed into a well-used road. Along this road they began to meet people and wagons laden with different goods. The road made its way to the edge of the forest and finally ended in a graveyard. Beyond it was the village. A sparse stand of birch trees[22] grew in the graveyard. Many crosses stood on the graves, most of them weathered from the rain and the sun. There were some yellowish-white crosses made from freshly cut wood. Andrew crossed himself from force of habit, but caught himself immediately. Immediately he felt slightly embarrassed in the depth of his soul for having a pang of conscience. His soul was not at peace. For too long he had served God. He had somehow become accustomed to his essence.[23]

On the edge of the graveyard Andrew saw a small group of people. The man and the woman stood still, and another man next to them was up to his waist digging. Andrew saw a small coffin. A tiny one. Seeing all this, he stopped dead in his tracks and could not keep his eyes off of what was going on.

The gravedigger had dug a grave. Expertly he picked up the coffin, put ropes under it, and holding it by the ends he began to lower the coffin to the bottom of the hole. A woman, who had been standing quietly, suddenly dropped to her knees. Andrew heard sobs mixed with laments. Her husband stood next to her, holding her up a bit and watched silently as soil falling from the edges of the grave was covering the coffin top and filling the void.[24] Andrew looked at the birch tree. Its branches were swinging rhythmically from soft wafts of air. He looked at the sky, the crows were converging on the village. He glanced at the road where people, cows and wagons were moving listlessly. Again he looked at the peasant and the woman, and at the gravedigger who was finishing his job. Pity choked his heart. Such a pity that his legs simply carried him toward the wretched couple. Suddenly, behind his back he heard peasants laughing. He turned around. The peas-

---

[21] devils in cassocks–an old curse

[22] birch trees – a symbol widely recognized as one standing for Russian nature, Russian soul and native culture

[23] essence–*ipostas'*, a church term, referring to one of the three faces of the Trinity

[24] began to lower the coffin to the bottom– During a Russian funeral the coffin is lowered into the grave, and it is covered with soil. The soil is piled on top so that it eventually forms a mound approximating the size of the coffin. This is all done in the presence of the mourners.

ants were walking, busy with their own conversation. A shout broke out in Andrew's soul: "A person has died! A person! Let everything be silent! Let all people be silent! Let the world say farewell to the person! He will never come to earth again!" But his shout was heard by no one.

The woman, oblivious to everything, was lying on the grave. Sobs were shaking her body. But where was the priest who should accompany the last voyage and give peace to the living? Andrew walked up to the gravedigger and quietly asked him about the priest.

– The infant had not been baptized. Didn't have time.

– Do they have other children?

– No, first born. They waited for him for a long time. He turned out to be not for this world.

Andrew looked at the man's face. It was severe, darkened. There was no pity for his wife in his face. Only his own personal pain was perceptible. Next to him, by his feet, the woman was still wasting away with grief.

Suddenly Andrew felt a wave of compassion flow over him. He surprised himself and walked right up to them, took off the cross from around his neck and holding it over the grave, he began to sing a psalm that no one had ever heard before. Words were born right there in his heart. He sang in his quiet and rich voice about sorrow not being sorrow, that the mother was right in lamenting this long awaited son as an angel. That he did become an angel, that God called him to Himself as a beautiful and pure child. That he will be happy in Paradise. That he will serve God with the other angels and pray for you, so that your life on this sinful earth is easier. And you, mother, need not grieve, simply be sad about your parting. There will be a time when you will see your wonderful child again.

Andrew's singing was heartfelt, and he tried to dispel the horrible darkness in the woman's soul. The peasant listened to him with the same severe look on his face. The woman became silent upon hearing the monk's voice. She looked at his serious face with surprise, lifted herself up onto her knees, and listened to these wondrous words while sobbing. Finally her face began to get lighter. For the last time Andrew made the sign of the cross over the grave and fell silent. The woman whispered quietly:

– Thank you, holy father.

– You will bear another child who will live on this earth.

He made a sign of the cross over her and went off toward the road.

ANSWER THE FOLLOWING

1. What is the main question or point of this story?
2. Describe Andrew's inner character and psychological state as presented by the narrator.

3. Describe the place where the action of this story occurs. How does it contribute to the main theme of the story?
4. Why did Andrew leave the monastery? Do you agree with the logic of his decision?
5. In your opinion, was he correct to take part in the burial of the child?
6. What is the role of organized religion in this story?

DISCUSS THE FOLLOWING

1. Is everything that is written in the Bible the truth?
2. Do people need religion to live honestly?
3. Is life in the monastery valuable and useful?
4. Is it correct if a person lies in order to make it easier for another person or make it more pleasant or less painful?
5. Do Andrew's arguments convince you?
6. Does Andrew believe in God at the end of the story?

COMMENTARY

INDISPUTABLY GOD IS ALL AROUND US

by Mikhail Dymarsky

The story is wonderfully kind and wise in its simplicity. Right before our eyes the defrocked monk who explains with such conviction why he has left the monastery and decided to part ways with God, turns into a priest, and what a priest! Into a priest who doesn't just drone on the necessary lines with indifference while at the same time thinking about lunch, but into an inspired one, one that can create and have compassion and grieve.

Contradictions in the Bible are an old theme. The questions which haunt Andrew and which finally lead him to leave God are no less old. Frankly speaking there is no particular valor in them, and to tell the truth, there is no particular wisdom in them either. One would have to be a very naïve person, or a very entrenched "bookworm," and an unbelieving one at that, to demand a lack of contradictions from the Holy Scriptures. As if all the authors of the Old Testament first got together and decided on all the details, and then they all went their separate ways, and each sat down to write their own book. No, Andrew's arguments are not convincing.

And they can't be convincing, since he himself does not understand what his soul has rebelled against. He says those horrible words "I hate all that is connected with God for he keeps me in darkness." But, who in reality has kept him in darkness? His own lack of faith.

And where should the faith come from, if, as he himself says, they gave him away to a monastery when he was just a baby? He didn't go there himself, but was "given away"! That's how he came to be an unwittingly naïve reader, one who tries to find formal logic where it cannot exist.

How naïve are man's vain attempts to part with that with which one cannot part! He "left" God, and immediately returned to him. But he returned a changed man. He returned because, maybe for the first time in his life, his soul was shaken by human sorrow. Because, maybe for the first time, he felt a REAL and HONEST need to turn to God, a need which neither he nor the parents who had been destroyed by sorrow, were aware of, but a need which as a result had become even more acute.

Andrew sings an unknown psalm, the words of which are born in his soul right there, over the tiny grave, and he cares not for logic in his text. He does not worry about the fact that even the act itself is not logical, since the infant had not been christened. Moreover, he cares not that at that moment, by his act he resurrects that which gives a beginning to all and that which he was not able to see, nor to understand, nor to feel during the long years of monastic life: the direct, ingenuous, real connection of man to God. Irrespective of the fact of whether or not he was christened, whether or not he believes, the connection exists. It is this connection that is at the foundation of religion, and everything else, books, churches, monasteries, all that is to one degree or another secondary.

The thankful characterization of the woman at the end of the story is deeply symbolic: "Thank you, holy father." It is the words "holy father" and not "unfrocked monk"! One can leave the monastery, but one cannot leave God – no. Having freed himself from the monastic duties, Andrew felt himself a free man. As it turns out, freedom is the shortest way to God.

The great Russian poet of the first half of the twentieth century, Aleksandr Vvedenskij, entitled his poems "It's possible God is all around". Having read Vladimir Monakhov's story, one wants to shout: INDISPUTABLY God is all around!

One is left to ponder – where will Andrew go now?

DISCUSS THE FOLLOWING

1. Do you agree with Dymarsky that this story is kind and wise?
2. Do you agree with Dymarksy's opinion of the questions which the monk asks himself?
3. In your opinion, is Dymarsky correct when he says that Andrew returned to God?
4. Do you agree that books, temples, monasteries, etc. are secondary?
5. Can you answer Dymarksy's question: Where will Andrew go now?
6. The question put forth in this story was also asked by such writers as Chekhov and Dostoevsky. Can you find parallels with this theme in Russian literature? In American literature?

A ROMANCE WITH A SEQUEL

Russian proverbs:

A chicken is not a bird; a woman is not a human being.
The more you beat your wife – the better the soup will be.
The hair is long, but the mind is short.

INTRODUCTION TO THE STORY

The position of Russian women in society has changed greatly over the centuries, as has the writing by Russian women authors. For many centuries the principles of Domostroj (*dom* house, *stroj* building; a text which provided the rules for everyday and domestic life) were strictly followed. This guiding work stressed the complete authority of the father and husband within the family. Nineteenth century Russia was a patriarchal, primarily agricultural, society in which women did the agricultural work, child bearing, child rearing, cooking, sewing and caring for the house. In the urban centers women had no economic security nor social rights, and although women of the merchant and noble classes had more social opportunities and some educational ones, they were still expected to obey their fathers and husbands. In fact, after marriage women were registered in their husbands' internal passports, and thus needed a man's permission to travel, work or study.

The 1860s brought many changes to Russia, including the emancipation of the serfs in 1861 and the first women's rights movement in Russia. Women won the right to obtain a secondary education and study at the university. In industry women's participation in labor rose considerably, while their salaries at the turn of the 20th century were one half to two thirds those of men.

The Bolshevik revolution in 1917 and its ensuing reforms gave women equal rights in all aspects of the new society; however, as Lenin stated, "Equality before the law does not automatically guarantee equality in everyday life."[1] Women were expected to be equals in the economic sphere while also being the bearers of the future citizens of the Soviet state. This placed a double burden on women: to be productive workers and productive creators, concurrently, in a country which placed light industry and domestic products a distant third to heavy industry and the military. Under Stalin family values were stressed as the strong foundation of society, and women were seen as the backbone of this foundation. Abortion was outlawed, and mothers with many children were hailed as "hero mothers of the Soviet Union."

During World War II women were needed in the war effort; they were necessary to maintain agriculture and industry while the men were fighting at the front. After the war many women were left widows, and thus there were many fewer men than women. Men were valued more (due to their scarcity), and women had to assume the traditional role of wife and mother, while still working (often as the head of the household). Many single mothers worked under dire economic and psychological stress.

In literature the portrayal of women has mirrored the position women have held or were expected to hold in society; under socialist realism women were characterized as "perfect and happy housewives and mothers, they were submissive and subordinate in their domestic role, and at the same time distinguished workers, fanatically loyal to their government and country."[2] Women writers presented women characters who were studying (political education), holding down jobs and becoming active in the new political system of the Soviet Union.[3] Women characters were shown as examples for the reader to follow and as examples of the changing position of women in the new society. During World War II women were portrayed as heroes, self-sacrificing for the cause. After the war women in literature were "strong and persevering, heroines not made of feminist convictions but of tragic circumstances."[4] After Stalin's death more attention was paid to private lives and individuals, male as well as female. Abortion was once again available

---

[1] As quoted in Helena Goscilo, *Dehexing Sex: Russian Womanhood During and After Glasnost* (Ann Arbor: University of Michigan Press, 1996), p. 8
[2] Sigrid McLaughlin (ed.) *The Image of Women in Contemporary Soviet Fiction* (New York: St. Martin's Press, 1989), p. 1.
[3] Catriona Kelly (ed.) *An Anthology of Russian Women's Writings, 1777-1992* (New York: Oxford University Press, 1994), p.. xiv.
[4] Sigrid McLaughlin., p. 2.

(and free to working women); however, women were still expected to work both outside the home and maintain the family within the home. Social themes of love (unrequited and tragic love) and the difficulties of life in the USSR were examined in works of literature (see Natalya Baranskaya's *Just Another Week* [*Nedelja kak nedelja*] a short novel which documents a week in the life of a Soviet woman of the 1960s.)

The protagonist of this story, "A Romance with a Sequel", written by Ilona Yakimova, is a woman who is judged by men, her lover and her editor. Both criticize her and her work, treating both as "immature," needing experience, which they characterize as needing to suffer, presumably at the hands of a man. The reader can see that she suffers in her relationship with her married lover, who has finally decided to leave his wife to marry her. Is this realistic? We will never know. However, her editor tells her that her work is not realistic, the dialogue is not realistic. The dialogue is that of her lover: is it realistic? Did it happen? Did he say these words? The protagonist presents herself as an independent woman, but as soon as a man criticizes her work, she quickly agrees to change it.

As Catriona Kelly explains, there is "…an urgent, anxious exploration of extreme psychological states"[5] of women in literature today. Two themes in Russian women writers' work are most prevalent (according to Catriona Kelly): "…a preoccupation with issues of autonomy" and "[the] tendency to realize this preoccupation by means of representation of a heroine who is both outstandingly gifted and a social misfit."[6] Ilona Yakimova's protagonist in this story is a writer (the reader may assume she is gifted) and, as the lover of a married man, a social non-conformist. She has tried to be independent; she does not answer "yes" immediately when her lover asks her to marry him. Thus, Yakimova's character embodies both of the themes Catriona Kelly ascribes to women authors in Russia today.

ILONA VLADIMIROVNA YAKIMOVA

THE AUTHOR ABOUT HERSELF

I live in the city of Gatchina. I was born in 1977 in Petrozavodsk in Karelia. I graduated from the Gatchina School-Institute (School #30), the physics mathematics class in 1993. In 1994 I entered St. Petersburg State Technological University of Plant Polymers majoring in ecological engineering. I entered graduate school in the field of the environment and rational use of natural resources. Since May, 2000 I also have been working as a junior

---

[5] Catriona Kelly, p. xv.
[6] *Ibid.*, p. xvi.

scientific research assistant in the branch of a scientific research laboratory of purification of industrial atmospheric waste, ecological management and marketing.

I have long been seriously fascinated by literature. I have taken part in the Literature Society under the leadership of Nonna Slepakova (St. Petersburg); 1995-1999 in the literary studio "Meridian" attached to the Palace of Culture in Gatchina (1999-2000), under the leadership of M. B. Kononov. Since 1999 I have been attending the Literary Society of Vjacheslav Lejkin.

I have been publishing since 1996 on a grant from a non-profit program "New Names," of the Russian Culture Fund since 1999 (poetry). Several times I have taken part in poetry evenings in Gatchina and St. Petersburg.

A ROMANCE[7] WITH A SEQUEL

by Ilona Yakimova

1997, GATCHINA, RUSSIA

Summer, July and the sun. I wonder if I have ever cared less about the fact that it was summer? Actually summer is enough in and of itself: a minimum of clothing and prejudices, but to forget about freedom I need a stronger passion than just enjoying the good weather. Zavyalov's[8] arm hugs my shoulders, provides protection, and I can enjoy the bulge of his muscles and the star tattoo on his forearm because he's wearing his least favorite gray jacket just for me and the short summer sleeves can be turned up. He has forgotten why he got this tattoo; I suspect just for pure pretentiousness, but he assures me–youthful indiscretion. Maybe in a couple of years he will forget me just as easily, as a middle age indiscretion, and he won't be able to find the reason that had propelled him into this amusing romance. But for now I have no intention of torturing him with questions such as is he happy or is he just playing with me.

July is burning our faces.

– May I kiss you?

– Do you really want to?

– Really.

– Then you may.

Pasha[9] bends toward me without missing a step, the wind sprinkles his forehead with whips of straw. We exchange a smile and a quick kiss–a fleeting kiss, therefore totally without sin. We have to hurry and before the end of July squeeze in a couple of days from the disappearing summer,[10] and we skid along the quickly moving, smooth day, tripping over yesterday's puddles....

And I wake with this warmth on my lips.

---

7 Romance–the Russian word in the title is *roman*, which in colloquial Russian can mean "a romance" as well as "a novel".

8 Zavyalov–last name based on the Russian root *v'-j* meaning "to wind down," "to fade", "to droop", "to wither"

9 Pashka, Pasha, Pashenka, Pash–all diminutive versions of the name Pavel, each carrying a tone of endearment.

10 disappearing summer–the story takes place in Northern Russia, close to the city of St. Petersburg, where the summers are short.

A two-meter giant, broad as a barrel, nose broken in a fight and in his eyes–the April sky. My mother shakes her head, "Look at his hands... He is not a man, but a wild animal. What's going to happen to you if you fall out of love with him?" A wild animal with great strength, I agree, but that's a compliment; as to what will happen if I fall out of love with him, it's not hard to tell, the result will be wretched. But I'm not too afraid of him, that is I'm not afraid at all. There is something child-like in Zavyalov, something fragile, almost feminine, tormented by submission and striving to deify the object of his passion. I command–great, that's just what he's waiting for: to caress me, to spoil me, to drown me in gifts, flowers and letters, letters uncharacteristic for his age filled only with unending rapture. Zavyalov is forty, and it may be that he sees in me a reflection of his disappearing youth. It seems that I can even break his very soul with one insistent glance... Eagerly I soar onto the pedestal. However, it soon turns out that "my monster"[11] is not as simple as it would appear. I find myself trying to figure out why it is that I need him, and I don't want to get into a long-lasting relationship, but our friends already set us up at parties. My mother gets the shakes from my new infatuation, but Zavyalov makes insinuations about the seriousness of his intentions, he can be devilishly charming, and most importantly, can appear absolutely innocent, just like a calf.

– Pashka, what would you do if I left you? Would you choke me, like Othello?

In his light eyes a smile flickers:

– I have no idea, haven't given it a thought. But as it stands, that's not a bad thought.

He lies. He would not raise a hand to me, this wild animal with an open heart.

Zavyalov is an actor, whose professional habits are second nature, and he can multiply his personalities. Sometimes I lose count in trying to figure out his real features. However, he won't play Hamlet. The Danish prince's skin cracks on his shoulders, but a fistfight–go for it. Robert Artois, Kaliban, Cashel Byron, Danton[12]–these are the roles that brought him fame,

[11] my monster–the Russian *izverg* means monster, but carries an endearing tone.
[12] Robert Artois, Caliban, Cashel Byron, Danton–Robert Artois is a character in Moris Druone's novel *Damned Kings*. The novel was adapted into a play, a scene edition, and produced at a local theater. Caliban is a character (a savage and deformed slave) in Shakespeare's "The Tempest." Cashel Byron is the main hero of George Bernard Shaw's novel *Cashel Byron's Profession* (1882). A stage production of this novel, in which Zavyalov starred, was called "The Career of a Certain Fighter." The role of Danton was played by the hero in a stage production of a Polish writer's story named "The Business of Danton." The production was inspired by Andrzej Wajda's film (*Danton*, France,1982) based on the same literary text. Yakimova explains that Zavyjalov's popularity was simply a consequence of his likeness to the main character in the film.

he is universal in his bear-like plasticity. Girls lose themselves in a surplus of tenderness in his eyes.

I seldom go to see him in the theater, since in a crowd of fifteen enthusiastic female admirers of a provincial theater, I look a bit cold.

Zavyalov very rarely takes the trouble to be interested in my literary talent as well. In his opinion I myself am the most valuable creation I should be proud of, with the exception of the unassuming musicality of my lyrics. By the way, he magnanimously gives me the right to hope for a wonderful future, and considers that I just haven't had enough bums in my life–the kind of jolts that can be engendered by strong passion or by horrible baseness. If only he had known how right he was … At least he would have refrained from such rash statements. In any case, we meet seldom enough for him to have time to work and for me to endow my creative loneliness with an illusion of fulfillment. He travels around the country, and when filming interrupts the tour, he comes home exhausted. Home which has more warmth than honesty and which demands totality from a woman. I, on the other hand, am outside the family, I, as before, enjoy poisoning Bohemian parties with a Mephistopheles' smile. I'm not the one who hangs my life around his neck, with touring and his letter writing and hysterics. Just the fact that Zavyalov considers my reporter's earnings nonsense gives me cause to reject all his attempts at ownership. He sends letters from all his trips, he does not demand marriage, worrying that with age he will become a burden to me. He is an unusually comfortable man. I prefer not to think about loving him. I find myself thinking that this relationship has a dual purpose; the second one being to learn the details of an affair between a married actor and a young provincial poetess. Kolya Granich, my old friend and a recently appointed editor, once said that my indescribable esthetics of the absurd are good for what I do, but dangerous for my life.

But I can't stop. The absurdity of this situation simultaneously makes me laugh and repels me. I can restrain any passion, no matter how tremendous, just for the sake of two hours of tedious work on a text. And there, having painstakingly come up with various expressions, I giggle and cry over those pages of love which I send to Zavyalov's touring return address with a dose of melancholy and a sad desire for tenderness...

There are three sensations in poetry: you lie, you tell the truth, and you are totally silent. I'm incapable of being silent.

I open the door. In the semidarkness of the entryway on the mirror, there is a note from my mother announcing what I should do today. A month ago Zavyalov had taken off on tour–it seems again to the Saratov[13] region

---

[13] Saratov–an important river port on the Volga, a medium size city with a population of under a million.

– and it's been almost a week without any news from him. That's not his style at all. Let him just show himself! Bloodthirsty plans for revenge float in my head alternating with my mother's instructions. While studying her list I feel someone's eyes on my back, not a heavy stare, but a tenacious one. Slowly I turn around; having made himself quite comfortable in the chair, Zavyalov is staring at me. In this pose he takes up a good half of the room:

– Well, hello.
– Where did you get a key?

He has no intention of hiding his grin:

– You mean you didn't lose it?
– Pashka!

No use being indignant. In some things he is openly stronger and has no need for my permission. All power is ephemeral. I skirt the chair just outside his reach, since I am sure that he himself will not get up; he's lazy, likes his comfort. But at the same time I knock off the table a bouquet which he had brought; a little extra nastiness never hurts, particularly since I plan to stay angry. Without turning Zavyalov follows my movement and, when I tug at his light brown hair, he obediently moves his head back. I ask, my voice dripping with honey:

– So, how were the Urupinsk[14] girls?

He opens his trusting eyes widely; a Godlike trinity and all sorts of poetry:

– What are you talking about?
– About the most important thing, Pashenka.

Of course, I'm not as mad as I would like to appear, but, nevertheless: not a word from him in a week, and here he just suddenly appears and is ready to talk about eternity. So that means that God only knows when he came back from the tour. Although Urupinsk is no Los Angeles, something drives me mad just in the fact that this city exists. No sense in making Zavyalov report on his activities; this would be, at best, a developed variation of a phrase I know all too well: "Business, little one!" Let's give the right to get all the details to his latest wife. She had stopped by a couple of days ago; who in the world had the gall to give her my address! The conversation was unusually thoughtful; that is to say, she is ready to do anything to preserve the family, and you–everything is still ahead and he–a grown man, a serious man, and you won't be able to hold on to him, I know that, that's why I got married; for you, young lady he is just a game... Alya, quiet, pleasant,

---

[14] Urupinsk–a small town in the Volgograd oblast, a stop on the Khoper River.

somewhat humiliated–exactly the opposite of me: a fig in the pocket[15], a knife at the bosom,[16] but it's this difference that fills my soul with dastardly superiority. Neither vanity nor love has mercy. It is my chair that Pashka Zavyalov is sitting in, it is me whom he's trying to embrace. Alya, you're probably right: your husband is just a fun game in my life...

The expression on my face must have changed at this point, and Zavyalov notices immediately:

– What's wrong? Did something happen?

A familiar way of needling:

– No, nothing in particular. It's just that my mother thinks that I need a boyfriend... closer to my age, that is, one less rough.

But, Zavyalov is not perturbed.

– No problem. My son has just turned fifteen, you want me to introduce you?

– Get lost, Pa-pa-sha[17], I have no intention of robbing the cradle.

I notice Zavyalov's palm making its way gently under my shirt.

– Paws!–I command ruthlessly.

No reaction. By the way, I would have been surprised had he reacted. Hey, Pasha, my gentle soul... I don't even care when in certain circles they refer to me as "the favorite." And when he lifts me up in his arms, I don't object; a usual prelude. He's lifted me up in his arms–which means that he's still thinking where to drop me. Such a romantic. It would be a sin not to rest in such arms; I feel an overwhelming need to pour out my sorrow:

– You know, again I was rejected by the editors... And Kolya said–not enough life experience.

– We'll get you some–promises Zavyalov, tilting his head toward my face.

– He's a creep, isn't he?

– He is, little one,–he gives a little smile.–Now be quiet!

Our further communication is in silence, and I just manage to remember that at the start of this conversation I was terribly angry with Zavyalov, and why is it that being so big and tough, he can be so tender, that Kolya is mistaken in thinking that I am lacking in life experiences, that by Monday I'll have to muddle through the story... Only after the fact do I notice my

---

[15] "a fig in the pocket"–lit. a gesture with the thumb between the index and the next finger, fist closed . This expression became popular in the nineteenth century after Saltykov-Schedrin's satirical writing scoffing at the person who never says openly what she thinks, because of her cowardice.

[16] knife at the bosom–a reference to a street-smart person with a certain amount of bravado

[17] Pa-pa-sha – a play on words using the hyphenated version of the endearing form of "father" and of Zavyalov's name, Pasha. The first two syllables actually spell "papa".

own moan.

The phone is ringing off the hook–somewhere on another planet. I'm warm and lost in stroking Zavyalov's tangled hair:

– Pash, you're staying, aren't you?

– Of course.

But I know he's looking at his watch.

How long have we been together, and why am I still with him–I've no idea. I'm not interested in certainty. There's no teary gentleness, no pity, no desire for a joint place of abode, it doesn't even occur to me; only haughty lips and the unclear sound of broken glass. And you would think, what could be simpler–just once to ask him to stay longer.

– You know, better return my letters...

How he looked at me, his look like the burn of a lash. A wolf, but I feel admiration even for this tone of a wild animal.

– Why?

– You want Alya to read them?–I ask calmly.

At the mention of his wife he becomes defenseless, for a minute, and then he narrows his eyes, pensively searching my face for something resembling a woman:

– Sometimes I think, girl, that you are false through and through, but I do love you precisely for the purity of that falseness. Even now you are choosing your words–just in case, to be able to substitute for the words I'm using. Might it come in handy some day? And the letters... not one correction, dictation on an assigned topic. Even in the rush of emotion you are incapable of using the wrong preposition or a wrong verb form! Better not write at all...

He bends over toward me, lifts my chin and turns my head toward the light, and toward himself:

– But that's not love.

I keep quiet. I don't know any other love, and he can't find compassion in my eyes, which are closing from the sun's sprays. I make Zavyalov both furious and helpless, and my words hurt him:

– And if I die tomorrow, you will write a poem based on that motif, right?

– A romance with a sequel–quietly and politely I define it more precisely. Epistolary.

There is something primordial in his rage, something worth seeing. But I don't get pleasure from torturing people and for a long time, I have not been capable of this and so, I admit honestly:

– No longer than ten lines–I promise.

More one can't promise even to God himself.

And Zavyalov knows that, and he has to agree; it's easier to come to a compromise than to deprive himself of me. And that's that. And it would seem what could be simpler than, just once, to stay longer... But here he is, already in the entry way, smoothly putting his jacket on, and if only I could hold on to that arch of his brows and to the dull gold of an unruly strand of hair falling into his eyes and to my own childish naivete departing with him... If only my hands were stronger. But again Zavyalov looks at me and just can't understand: am I sorry to have to let him go or am I looking for a rhyme for the word "postmodernism"? And at that moment he simply hates me and kisses me goodbye. And I, hanging on his strong neck, laugh, because he hurts and caresses the same way.

I almost flatter myself. Having secured me for himself completely, together with all the eulogies, translations, midnight watch and all sorts of humanitarian nonsense, Pasha immediately attempts to clip my wings and shove me into the chicken coop. He's in love with the aura of a free spirit, living just on words, but the submissiveness of other women engenders Satrap passion[18] in him. He's not the first, and he won't be the last to be so attractively mistaken. Even so, for some time now he has begun to look at other people's children with a certain amount of disquietude, and tries to find in me the prerequisites of a family woman, but I'm in no hurry.

– Marry me.

Cold, sober eyes. It appears that only now he has defined me as an object to be conquered. Now he won't retreat. Just another aspect of Zavyalov that I have to deal with.

– Pashka,–I surmise.–Have you lost your mind?

That should be expected. Two wild forces mingle into a bundle, and I cling to my freedom with the ferocity of youth. But suddenly, instead of just breaking me, he moves on to arguments–and he talks, and entices... So, it's as if I had agreed and was just waiting for justification for my agreement: he's not a monster, and indeed, whoever said it's only in fiction...? We will be a great couple, he loves me... And all such nonsense that thrills the "walk-ons" of his troupe. His strength is that earth-shattering sky in his eyes, that fragility that comes with an abundance of strength, that open heart placed at my feet, that's where his strength is. He loves me, that's true, he loves me selflessly. And in this selflessness he can kill with his love. Only when is he finally honest: now he's tender, yesterday furious, and heartless half an hour ago? He barely knows his own face. And I, when should I consider

---

[18] Satrap passion – a reference to an ancient despotic Iranian governor who had total judicial control and collected taxes. Here, this implies suffering.

myself true: loving him in the name of poetry, writing poetry in the name of my love for him? You can spend a century, mixing up days, actors' faces, fragments of verses and lives. New face, new eyes. It would be better if you didn't look at me like that, Pasha, much better...

– Tomorrow you're leaving for Moscow, right?

– Right.

I ponder Zavyalov's face, move my hand over it, pluck at it, drinking in the flesh of his closed eyelids and lips. Have I ever had next to me such a person who has himself forged a collar with such ecstasy?

– Call me when you get back.

– At night?

– No matter. You won't wake anyone but me... And then I will answer you. He leaves with a promise of an end, shedding its familiar taste of summer. I taste the traces of warmth on my lips. Already I know that I will say "yes" when he calls, and even more, I know that I will have to pay for it dearly. You can't reach the same heaven twice.

At night I actually do say "yes", and the barely audible hoarseness of broken sleep only adds a charm to the voice, and then I dream of summer, July, his arm, encircling my shoulders, and all our love, sunny, playful, a bit ephemeral, an amusing romance with a sequel. And already I don't care what people will say, how words which suffer no tyranny will treat me, how we will get used to living together—intoxicated by the omnipotence of love. I leave all these questions for "after the wedding." His protection and my complete serenity that I so loved in Zavyalov—he who has not even once in his life dared to dream is dead.

The ring of the phone in the empty apartment scrapes along my nerves —lengthwise and a bit on the diagonal. Stumbling into objects, floating in the milky white of the morning light, I finally find the receiver:

– They killed Zavyalov!

Not making out the caller's voice, I slowly drop to the ground. I'm not hysterical, I simply don't hear anything. Details flow into one abominable mirage, and I only know one thing; they had cut out his heart with a switch-blade. The person who had done this didn't even suspect who it was that he had murdered, and two hours after our conversation Pasha died in the street, and until five o'clock he lay there looking through the morning sky, in vain trying to concentrate... I can't help it, but Zavyalov appears to me lying flat on his back, unnaturally helpless, with his chest ripped open. I'm feeling nauseated, and I retch in the bathroom, retching up all the love mixed in with bile. But no tears—I cried them all out in childhood, crying about broken dolls. Time to live like an adult.

He died—what a vile trick, trite and vile. He died just when I trusted him so well, when I dared to hope. He died and left me in blinding loneliness, having promised too much, to one so mature for her age. I won't again believe in the immortality of man. Hundreds of words said in vain, he will never know how I love him. A black line of blood on my wrist, it clots, just another disappointment. Everything in life must be done competently.

And later, at the funeral, I will stand a bit in the distance, and my frozen face will only serve as an extra reason for passing judgment, and the lawful widow, proud in her mourning, will consider the appearance of the out of wedlock widow as a clear impropriety. And so was the last time that I saw Zavyalov, last—because not even in the most absurd of hopes do I ever look into the sky. The sky is indifferent to us. Admit it, Pashenka, you left me no choice. All I have left are the letters. Instead of a cigarette I chew on words, words that fly out of my lips, feeling the burned taste of philological blood in my mouth. And try to foretell what will happen faster: will the commuter train come first or will I sign an agreement? It's only a matter of time. When I sit down to write in my lap, looking out the window, the last lights swim away. And Zavyalov is left alone in the cooling city, able neither to change course nor to hold...

Kolya Granich is a treasure when sober, when drunk he's the king of the men of letters, and now I need him to be inspired. He didn't know Zavyalov personally—that's his biggest attribute, and because of that I even feel it necessary to visit him at the dacha. Kolya opens the door, absolutely sober and sorrowful, but right from the start I reject any condolences, and something flickers in his eyes; something like a stale surprise at this late visit, or something like admiration for the cruelty with which I conquer my fallen passion.

Outside the windows you can hear the damp singing of the night garden. I fan the pages out onto the table, without a smile I answer the silent question:

There haven't been any like this since Laclos'[19] Epistolarian romance ... and I add with hesitation. – With a sequel.

Quickly glancing over a few pages, Kolya raises his catlike eyes, he can always find the main point at a glance. And I begin to get tangled in a sticky, syrupy Granich web.

– Actually, I expected this for a long time now. You are beginning to leave the diaper stage—it's time to... It's strong, stylistically passable, but the vain attempts at psychology—I'm sorry. Love is not fashionable these

---

[19]   Laclos—Pierre Choderlot de Laclos (1741-1803), a French writer, the author of a famous (at the time) epistolary novel *Dangerous Connections* (1782)

days. And, on top of that, this kind of love. Here's a good paragraph... but, tell me, please, where ever did you hear of a healthy forty-year-old man using such expressions about love, in our time, such expressions? Was he this obtuse? You can see that this is the naiveté of a schoolboy.

Turning his birdlike profile to me, enveloped in clouds of cigarette smoke, Granich pronounces a verdict:

– It's not too believable!

" ... Summer, July and the sun... Zavyalov's arm encircling my shoulders..." And here I grin. A stupid, crooked grin, unwittingly crawls all over my face.

– I'll rewrite it. I swear, Kolenka[20]

But he has no intention of being surprised. Instead Granich, coldbloodedly bound by hospitality, shoves a glass in my hand, above the edges of which delirium flutters in alcohol fumes.

It's sometimes interesting to expose what goes on behind the scenes of a given career.

By the way, the first two years were horrible. Having returned from Granich and finding mother having her morning coffee, still a bit unnerved by Zavyalov's trick, I exhibited my interest scrupulously: "So are you happy? Now he'll never be able to kill me, never." They considered it a normal symptom of depression. At first I returned home apprehensively, particularly when I was not alone, and I would stare at the empty chair. I was not afraid of Pasha. But he could just as well have appeared if only to see the expression on my face. Now I have moved the chair further away from the entrance. I no longer turn to see an intent stare at my back. Zavyalov has become a dim anguish over the unfulfilled, over a mocking smile, over the only power able to break me. Time will pass, and I will return to stand at his grave. And if now and again I suddenly lose the thread of conversation, if the names of those I speak with flow into one strange name, it is certainly not because of an unhappy love. Only these dreams, they keep coming back every other night. I'm tired of these whispers behind my back, of advice to get more rest, of these good wishes. My memory is corrupted, it harbors that which others have long ago disowned. Recently I have become fond of water, very fond, with no ulterior motive. Maybe it's not as cold as they say... And sometimes I ask men who happen to be nearby to roll up their sleeve, but I have not seen a single star on a forearm.

Time moves on. Even in death one can find something resembling life.

---

[20] Kolenka —diminutive of Kolya, which is a nickname for Nikolai

Strands of light fall onto the forehead and mingle with hair, eyes acquire the shade of honey-or is it the sun making its way into the curtain slits, breaking against the window frame, or is it the old dream coming back like the even beat of an illness left untreated? Warmth on the face... Why is it that those feelings in dreams possess such torturous authenticity?

And I wake with this warmth on the lips.

For ten years I've been waking with this warmth on my lips.

ANSWER THE FOLLOWING

1. Describe the characters of this story.
2. What role does the artistic process play in this story?
3. Do you think that for a successful result of the artistic process one needs to have extensive life experience, especially hardship?
4. How would you react if you were the mother of the writer of this story?
5. What role does Zavyalov's being an actor play?
6. Do you think that there is a difference between the given type of a young Russian poetess and a typical young American poetess? Can one use the word "typical" when discussing a poet?
7. Who is Granich and what role does he play in this play?

DISCUSS THE FOLLOWING.

1. Discuss the relationship of the narrator and Zavylov from the point of view of the narrator.
2. How would Zavyalov himself describe the relationship?
3. How does the narrator behave after Zavylov's death?
4. How would the story change if it were written by a man?
5. Who would like this story more, a man or a woman? Why?
6. While reading the story, do you feel that the author is a poetess? (Use specific examples from the text.)

COMMENTARY

THE PRICE OF A DREAM

By Mikhail Dymarsky

Ilona Yakimova's story is written with burning honesty and wisdom. It is characterized by the very qualities of contemporary "women's prose," which has blossomed in Russia in the second half of this century: unity of deep felt feelings, unattainable by men, with precise intellectuality.

"Romance with a Sequel" is not devoid of a certain dose of mystery. On the one hand, if we are to depart a bit from the artistic fabric of the text itself, the *sjuzhet*[21] of the story can seem too simple, almost childishly naive. A young girl falls in love with a mature and almost ideal man, and all obstacles on the path to their mutual feelings just disappear. They are about to decide to marry (and for him this means a decision to leave his current wife), and just at this point, for some strange and unknown reason, he is murdered, and she treasures her feelings and does not forget him for ten years. It appears that this *sjuzhet* holds more of a dream than that which we have come to call "real life." What girl has not dreamed of such love that would make her and her chosen one forget all else, make them conquer all obstacles and even sacrifice life itself in the name of feelings? What girl has not see herself in the role of a heroine treasuring as holy the faithfulness of lost love?

On the other hand, the naiveté and unrealistic qualities of the *sjuzhet*, for some reason, are not irritating. So what that it is naive and not probable? Maybe at the basis of the *sjuzhet* lies a dream and not a story in which we should believe according to the rules of the game? Or maybe the ideal qualities of the *sjuzhet* are balanced by the "absurdity of the situation" which "mocks and repels at the same time", a situation, the essence of which can be, as it turns out, summed up as follows: "an affair between a married actor and a provincial poetess," love, where each of them has their own professional interest(!). Finally, it may be that the story is written in fast-paced, lively and witty dialogues balanced on the edge of pathetic seriousness and deadly irony, including self-irony.

Then what is this story about?

At first reading one somehow does not take note of the elegance of its circular composition: at the beginning, as well as at the end, the same dream is mentioned, but how different is the modal coloration of each! One does not even notice that the events had taken place in the distant past; in the second sentence of the text the main character of the story poses a rhetorical question: "I wonder if I have ever cared less about the fact that it was summer?"–and now it is clear that more than one year has passed. And the reader, forgetting all this, is almost amazed when at the end the heroine discloses that "For ten years I've been waking with this warmth on my lips."

---

[21] *sjuzhet*–Although *sjuzhet* is often translated as "theme", to the formalists, such as Tomashevsky, it was distinct from the theme and from the plot. One possible translation is "story;" however, the use of the word *sjuzhet* is also accepted. In the formalist interpretation *sjuzhet* is the schematic arrangement of a given work, the order in which the author places those episodes and scenes that advance the theme or the idea behind the given work. In this context Dymarsky uses it to mean "theme."

Of course one of the secrets of this effect is in the skillful use of verbal forms in the "present epic" tense which create the illusion of convergence of the narrative to the present time for the reader, and even to the peculiar Russian version of the English "Future in the Past." "And later, at the funeral, I will stand a bit in the distance..." But that is not the only reason. The primary secret lies in the fact that throughout the entire text the reader's attention is so artfully held by those layered weavings of feelings–thoughts and wishes–rejections of both of the characters and in the fact that the reader just does not expect such an absurd and stilted end to the *sjuzhet*. In addition, when this end does take place, the story does not end. It is then that the reader's attention is unwittingly refocused onto the details, onto the style of writing, onto individual remarks which the narrator drops so "accidentally" along the path of narration, without, it would appear, too much attention as to their appropriateness or connection to the *sjuzhet*.

The heroine-narrator writes poetry, and this is what determines her view of the world. For her, as opposed to the reader and a "regular" person in general, there is no boundary line between poetry and life because art is the inseparable and the central part of her life. Her life flows into poetry, and she views life itself as poetry. It is from poetry that the story is filled with distant rhymes: "There are three sensations in poetry: you lie, you tell the truth, and you are totally silent," – says the heroine, and two paragraphs later we find the following phrase: "He opens his trusting eyes widely; a *Godlike trinity and all sorts of poetry*" [italics M.D.]. It is from poetry that she takes her use of play on words. Just look at how the story works its title.

In actuality the story is not about love, but about that "impetus," which in Zavyalov's opinion is "lacking" in the heroine and which will open for her "a luxurious future." Luxurious, of course, not in the material sense and worldly goods, but in the sense of a career in literature. That is why, at the end of the story, she drops a bitter phrase: "It's sometimes interesting to expose what goes on behind the scenes of a given career."

A literary career means success. Kolya Granich's lessons have not been in vain, but most importantly – the demanded price has been paid. It appears this is the way we are to understand the phrase: "And try to foretell what will happen faster: will the commuter train come first or will I sign an agreement?" This phrase surprises the reader in a paragraph that begins with a description of the funeral. What agreement? It may be the notorious pact with the devil, but the role of the devil-temptor is played by art. Having not recovered from a shock the heroine "sits down to write on her lap"...

This is what this story is about. Not about love, not about a dream, but about that terrible price which is paid by an artist for her service to art.

She pays with what is most dear to her, with what she has: those whom she loves and herself. She dies in her art and what is left is just a "resemblance of life" ("Even in death one can find something resembling life.") For example, to wake with a deceiving warmth on the lips.

The idea, like the situation, is not new. But this fact does not diminish the pain...

It is this pain, which unwittingly seeps through the pages with its bloody spots, that is most valuable in "Romance with a Sequel." That is why the honesty of its restrained narration is so burning.

DISCUSS THE FOLLOWING

1. Dymarsky thinks that on one level the story is simple and naïve. He thinks that the girl has fallen in love with the ideal man. Do you agree?

2. Dymarsky believes that the naïvete of the *sjuzhet* is not irritating. Do you agree?

3. Do you agree with Dymarsky's opinion that this may be self-irony?

4. Dymarsky thinks that for the heroine/narrator there is no difference between poetry and life. Do you agree?

5. From Dymarsky's point of view this is a story not about love, but about the "impetus" which is lacking in the narrator's literary career. Do you agree?

6. How does Dymarsky explain the phrase "And try to foretell what will happen faster: will the commuter train come first or will I sign an agreement?" Do you agree with his interpretation?

7. Do you agree with Dymarsky's conclusion with regard to the theme of this story?

RELIC

INTRODUCTION TO THE STORY

Russia began to discover and explore Siberia under Ivan IV (Ivan the Terrible, 1533-84) when a gateway to the east was opened as he extended the power of Russia's rule beyond ancient Rus', thus creating the beginning of a multi-national empire. Westward expansion continued as Siberia (the land east of the Ural Mountains) became a "wonderland" for explorers, hunters, trappers, mining prospectors and traders. Siberia offered unimagined wealth to those willing to brave the harsh climate. In addition, Russia established military ports and outposts while it reached towards the Pacific coast which it reached in 1649. Due to its vast expanse of land (and the subsequent difficulty in governing such a large area) those seeking religious freedom and escaped serfs saw Siberia as a safe haven. The tsarist government also used Siberia as a vast prison, sending those whose political views were critical of the regime out of European Russia, away from the population centers. In later years under Soviet rule Siberia became a locale for the prison system, known as the Gulag.

Siberia is a land of great resources, albeit it has been difficult to reach these resources due to the northern location and the subsequent cold climate and frozen land. Indigenous populations learned to live on the land, without creating major environmental problems, since they only needed to hunt and fish in order to live. When more modern "explorers" came to Siberia, they were looking for the riches to be found both in the animals and in the ground in the form of ores and other natural resources. As Stalin pushed to industrialize the Soviet Union at an accelerated pace, the incentives to extract more and more from the land were increased. The Soviet Union's urgent need for ore to produce steel to build its industrial base, as well as its need for minerals (e.g. gold, diamonds, etc.), resulted in exploration being carried on with little or no regard for the environment. Siberia became a vast "warehouse" of "supplies" for the industrial might of the Soviet Union.

This exploitation can be seen in the vast areas of forests that were logged and left barren. It is only in recent years that a program of reforestation has been utilized. The fishing and pelt industries were overtaxed by the Soviet authorities, and after fishing with nets was no longer productive due to dwindling supplies, the invading Soviets used dynamite to collect the fish. Eventually, the government fishing industry depleted the supplies. Hunting for valuable pelts was moved to "fur farms" where the animals were raised for their fur. Native peoples, who had previously fished and hunted for food, could no longer support themselves.

Exploration for energy resources became very important as the industrial and population base of the Soviet Union expanded and became more dependent on energy. After extensive research, specialized methods for the extraction of energy products from the permafrost earth were successful, in that it was possible to extract the resources. The environmental damage was severe as little attention was paid to spills, leakage, and the destruction of the natural habitat of many native animals.

When the Russians and then Soviets came to Siberia, they saw themselves as the bearers of modern civilization to the backward native peoples, as they had seen themselves vis-à-vis the Russian peasants. Geoffrey Hosking discusses the portrayal of the peasant in Soviet literature; the peasants "… were to be modernized themselves–if necessary, dragged kicking and screaming into the socialist society whose rightness they themselves would all one day recognize."[1] The policy of "Russification" (and later "Sovietization") had no regard for the native customs, traditions and lifestyles of the Siberian people. Schools were set up in which Russian was the primary language, so that many native languages were lost as a result of disuse. In addition the "modern civilization" brought alcohol to the native peoples. As their traditional occupations were no longer able to sustain them, the people had to work for the Russians and Soviets who were exploiting the natural environment (often using prisoner labor.) As an added enticement to a people who had lost their traditional livelihood and their pristine environment, the Russians/Soviets brought alcohol, which they freely provided, to the depressed people.

---

[1] Geoffrey A. Hosking, "The Russian Peasant Rediscovered: 'Village Prose' of the 1960s" *Slavic Review*, 32 (1973), p. 707.

After the fall of the Soviet Union in 1991, when the country and its people gained access to the information of the Western world and vice versa, the population (both within the country and the scientific community abroad) began to have access to information that exposed the exploitation of the environment and the peoples of Siberia. Two questions were actively debated in the press, both in reference to the country as a whole and specifically to Siberia: Who is to blame? What is to be done? *Who is to Blame?* is the title of Aleksandr Hertzen's 19th century work while *What is to be Done?* is the title of Vissarion Belinsky's work of the same century. In Helena Goscilo's introduction to her anthology *Glasnost: An Anthology of Russian Literature under Gorbachev*, while speaking of the new freedoms of the *glasnost* era under Mikhail Gorbachev, she says, "Two cardinal questions repeatedly posed throughout the massive retrieval of bygone years recall the interrogative titles of two classic nineteenth-century novels that programmatically appealed to Russians' civic conscience..."[2] Russia is now asking these questions in reference to the country and its future, and one can see this underlying searching in the examination of the exploitation of Siberia and its native peoples.

The village prose movement in Russian literature of the 1950s and beyond looked at the "conflict between urban and rural life."[3] This prose examined how industrialization and urbanization had been destroying the peasants' rural life, his/her close relationship with nature.[4] Different aspects of this conflict are also examined in the literary work in this collection. Mikhail Butov uses Maksim, the main character of his story "Relic", as a man who was born into the rural life of a Siberian people, but who had to live and work torn between that life and that of the encroaching Soviets who had overfished Siberian waters, who had cut down trees to build the telegraph poles which led to a Siberian prison camp, who raped his wife, and had left him a relic of a bygone era. The question of responsibility is poignant in this story. Butov sympathizes with Maksim for Maksim is left a lonely man who no longer has a place in the "new Siberia," a land which the Russians/Soviets have used for years and have left as a legacy of "modernization" without regard for the traditions and lives of the native peoples.

---

[2]   Helena Goscilo and Byron Lindsey (ed) *Glasnost: An Anthology of Russian Literature under Gorbachev* (Ann Arbor: Ardis Publishers, 1990), pp xxiv-xxv.
[3]   Charles A. Moser (ed) *The Russian Short Story: A Critical History* (Boston: Twayne Publishers, 1986), p. 184.
[4]   Geoffrey Hosking, p. 712.

MIKHAIL BUTOV

ABOUT THE AUTHOR

Mikhail Vladimirovich Butov was born in Moscow in 1964. He graduated from an institution of higher technical education. Since 1992 he has published stories, tales, essays and articles in important literary publications in Russia. Two books of his have appeared. His works have been published in German, French and Korean. He is the winner of a series of Russian literary awards. In the year 2000 he won the Smirnoff-Booker prize for his novel *Svoboda* (*Freedom*) which was judged the best Russian novel of 1999. At the present time he is working as the executive secretary of the Russian literary journal *Novij mir*.

RELIC

By Mikhail Buton

LATE 1980S, MOSCOW, RUSSIA

Had someone taken enough interest in Maksim to ask him about his first memory, Maksim would have told them about the bear that had wandered into the village on the river Turukhan.[5] It was in the spring when families were coming back from migrant fishing work, and the village was again filled with people. The first bear was killed according to custom: the men stood in a circle around it and fired once each, wounding, but not killing him. Then, accompanied by the smiles of the hunters, his father gave him the rifle, but Maksim didn't have enough strength to hold it tightly so his father helped and held the barrel for him. The last shot was reserved for the oldest person, and for the rest of his life Maksim remembered the ancient, old woman, darkened with age who appeared completely decrepit but who, practically without taking aim, sent a bullet right into the animal's eye.

Since then there were many bears–Maksim could not even give an approximate number, he didn't think in such quantities. Many years later he was surprised to realize that those who taught him were gone, as well as those who learned alongside him, and that now he was the one who was the best at killing bears. Before, his father was the best, and as soon as Maksim was strong enough, he took him along when he went to the taiga.[6]

At that time he had not yet been Maksim. It was a name given to him by his Russian teacher[7] who had a passion for renaming everything around her, even lakes and meadows. His fellow classmates she christened with names like Ninelya and Rem.[8] The name she had chosen for him must

---

[5] Turukhan River–in Siberia a tributary of the Enisei, 639 km. long. A place of political exile during both Tsarist Russia and Soviet Union.

[6] taiga–the forest vegetation zone which stretches from the Gulf of Finland to Kamchatka. This area has been sparsely populated; the native peoples were hunters and gatherers. In European Russia some of the taiga has been cleared and used for agriculture.

[7] Russian teacher–During the Soviet period the official language in all Republics for all nationalities was Russian, although the native language was also accepted. The government sent Rusian teachers to most settlements.

[8] Ninelya, Rem–During the early years of socialism in the Soviet Union it was fashionable to give unusual names. Ninelya is Lenin spelled backwards with the addition of -ya to

have also reminded her of something revolutionary.[9] It was then that the Russians came, during the years when he became conscious of his own self. They opened a school and divided all the inhabitants into two groups, adults and children, in order to teach them to read and write. Vodka came with them. In a land where five or six dogs are eaten to death by black flies each summer they had a hard time with melancholy and drank anything that burned. Before it was strictly forbidden to sell alcohol to the Selkups[10] in the surrounding towns and villages, but now it was delivered right to their village.

Maksim liked going to school. He was indifferent to castles built in the air of a better future life,[11] for he could not comprehend how one could wait for some other life, one different from the one he was already living. He, however, was enchanted by the anticipated magic which he saw in everything the teacher talked about. He anticipated something like a fairy tale and yet realistic, something which was to happen right here, on the banks of the river from where his people had taken their genealogy.

Not everyone got along with the Russians, and with each year fewer and fewer families returned to their old place. Maksim stayed with his parents. They were already tied to the place by vodka, and being among strangers in general suited Maksim. He hung around with the Russian children, he managed their language better than they his. And so imperceptibly this language became his native, and he began to think in it, and he recalled his original name less and less frequently, particularly since his parents also quickly got used to the new one.

When the teacher began to tell them about some big war[12] going on somewhere, it seemed to Maksim that she was making it up; he could not imagine masses of people killing each other. But the teacher, and the majority of the Russians whom they all got used to, soon disappeared and all the Selkups, children and adults, were put to fishing. Every three days in the summer there came a boat and in the winter a strange machine with blades whirling in the air. A man in a leather coat with fur trim supervised the loading of the barrels and spreading his two fingers in front of him

make a female name. Russian readers would recognize this immediately. Rem is probably just a made up name.

[9]   something revolutionary–Many children were named after communist leaders, writers, events or accomplishments. Maksim was the first name of Gorky (1868-1936), whom many considered to be the father of Socialist Realism.

[10]   Selkups–a traditional name for the Ostako-Samoeds inhabiting the Tumen and Tomsk oblast in the Krasnoyarsk region

[11]   better future life–refers to Communist slogans which "advertised" a wonderful future to which all workers were to strive. "Castles in the air" obviously questions the reality of these dreams.

[12]   reference to World War II. The Russians call this war the "Great Patriotic War" .

shouted "More, you red skinned churki,[13] we need twice as much, got it?" Only in the third spring did he finally understand that you just could not get more with nets, and he started to bring dynamite. Now there were no fish left in the vicinity of the village, and they had to go away for a few days to come back with a catch. Those whom he considered to be better than others the guy in the leather coat rewarded with alcohol, and Maksim got as much as anyone.

He also heard vague rumors that this incomprehensible war had finally ended. Although the Selkups were not conscripted, their population in the town had become almost half as small as a result of winters spent on the ice without rest. Up the river they opened a meteorological station, and the men began to go there to trade pelts for vodka and bullets. These days people with knapsacks, rifles and objects whose usage Maksim could not even begin to guess, would appear in the town from time to time. They searched for something in the taiga, they themselves often remaining there forever, and Maksim would bump into remains left over by wild animals. Even then he was considered to be the best hunter and they all wanted to talk to him. Maksim would describe an area to them, shake his head and he'd repeat: "Why are you going there? Why die?" They'd laugh condescendingly. He learned to tell who would return and who would not.

The taiga had changed in a day. Barges floated down the Turukhan and people driven by other people got off them, people in clothing not suited to local conditions. They cut down trees, built long low buildings and stretched barbed wire along the poles. When they cut an opening in the forest, Maksim found out there would be a road, and that cargo would be transported along this road destined for construction in lands he had never heard of. One day several men in uniform came to the village, questioned the women and then knocked at his door. By then Maksim was alone: his mother faded away during the fishing period and his father froze to death when he got drunk and became lost in a snowstorm. He was beginning to languish in the village and immediately agreed to work for them. His duties consisted of every week walking the thirty-verst[14] line of telegraph poles and bringing to their attention any damage he noticed. Now he was surrounded by emaciated, barely alive people: they carried logs, pushed wheel-barrels up hills and hammered in piles into the frozen earth. Many of them perished. Maksim did not know about the place where other such people dug huge holes where they tossed in the bodies of the dead. It wasn't that he didn't

---

[13] Churki–a pejorative term for the indigenous people of the region
[14] verst – 1.0668 km.

question at all what fate could have thrown these people here, to this labor which surpassed their strength, and why others had such power over them, what kind of man was this, in his perception, he could not comprehend, because he saw how they killed openly and with no fear of revenge. But a certain folk wisdom whispered to him: that which is happening is so far outside his world view that even an attempt at understanding could be dangerous for him.

He became famous on the road. Administrators would come and get him when they had to entertain a highly-placed guest. These people were incompetent hunters, and deep in his soul Maksim despised them, and after one of them had the brilliant idea of dropping a moose with grenades, Maksim had to force himself to agree to go with them, but he did agree, feeling that to refuse would be dangerous.

This was when he got married. There was only one bride in the village, but her parents wasted no time in choosing to whom to give her in marriage. Maksim, being close to the higher-ups, appeared a suitable groom. When he took her home, he bought her a blue calico scarf in the camp store.

Then even these people disappeared. They left their barracks, kilometers of rusting rails and burial grounds, which soon grew over with underbrush. Those who had grown up in the village during the time of the construction followed them. A rumor had flown around that now they would settle the Selkups in cities. The only people left in the village were Maksim and a few old people. He also would have left, but not long before that, he bumped into a bear woken up by someone. He was without a rifle and, before he could get his knife into its heart, the bear managed to drop its paw onto his thigh. The bone was sticking out, but his wife saved him from infection by wrapping it in herbs, and the leg healed, but now it was bowed, turned inside out. Having given it some thought, Maksim decided he could not get along in the city in his condition.

Maksim's wife, having given him two children, began to grow into the ground. She used to be stately according to the standards of her people, but now she was getting smaller, so it seemed to him, smaller with each day. When the last half-Russian woman, Maria, went to die in the taiga, he moved his family to the closest house to the forest, the former school. The helicopters which had appeared over the taiga added nothing to his life. Those who flew on them stayed only for one season, leaving behind the still-assembled drilling derricks, and the fish left the river for two years.

One spring the children, while playing, got into one of his boats and didn't notice that the rope had untied. The current picked up the boat and in their fright they decided to jump out–the shore seemed to be close. Maksim pulled out their bodies, tangled in sedge far from their house, but he buried them right in front of the stoop and didn't decorate the graves. They just stayed there, two grassy little hills.

After the winter two men appeared in his house. Who they were he never did find out. They were well-fed, strong, they cursed scathingly, and they poured him spirits,[15] so that later all he could do was cower pitifully in a corner and watch what they did to his wife. He came to when they collected all the rifles and nets in the house and were getting ready to leave. He managed to get out unnoticed, got his double-barrel shot gun which he had hidden in his boat, and he emptied two bullets into their heads. Then he put the corpses up onto the net dryer poles to keep the animals away and he walked; all the dogs had died from a disease brought by the oil workers' dogs, and there were none to be harnessed. He walked to Krasnoselkup.[16] He made it there in a week and a half and having arrived at night he knocked at the first house and asked where the mayor lived. Within three days he was delivered home, already from Turukhansk, by a helicopter, and they made him show them where they all had been standing, then they shoved him back in the helicopter and flew him away. They took the frozen corpses and confiscated all his rifles. Maksim returned eight years later, and he didn't even tell his wife what had happened to him during the time he was gone. And she had become completely small, no taller than a child. Without him she ate only what fell into the scrap of a net that she set up right where the path from the house went into the water. Her legs had stiffened, and each step brought her pain.

In the surrounding world Maksim found only one change: it was easier to exchange pelts. People at the trade station appeared to have stopped being afraid of that which they used to fear. For a time people even came around buying up pelts for money, and Maksim was able to order himself a metal boat and a motor for it.

Tourists came now instead of geologists, more and more of them were attracted by the Road of Death.[17] To Maksim they all looked alike: they all just could not believe that he lived there alone, that he traveled using dogs in the winter and that he could hunt bear with a boar spear. Maksim showed them the camps falling into decay. Some left something: tea, pepper.[18] They all just had to take a picture of him and his wife, and

---

[15] spirits–stronger than vodka, pure alcohol
[16] Krasnoselkup–*krasnyj* is Russian for red. Thus, the town was named "Red Selkup," red being the symbolic color of the Soviet Union.
[17] Road of Death–This is a reference to a road traveled by labor camp prisoners. Many prisoners died along such roads.
[18] Tea and pepper were items that were not readily available in Siberia; however, for the Russians who left them, these items were of no consequence.

they promised to send copies to him in care of the meteorological station. Not one of them ever did.

His wife still lived a long time, although she almost didn't move around at all on her numb legs. Maksim began to have trouble sleeping at night, and he stared at her midget-like figure. One morning he didn't find breath in her, but he didn't immediately figure out what had happened, since so little life had been left in her body for the past few years. Fish needed drying, and he decided to bury her later, when he had finished, but he didn't want to leave her in the house so he brought her out onto the steps. In the cot in which she had been sleeping Maksim found the blue scarf, the one he had bought her for their wedding.

When he returned from the shore, the body was gone from the steps. Judging by the trampled grass and a break in the bushes, Maksim figured out that the bear had been big, he had not seen such a big bear in these lands before.

It wasn't that he finally understood something, or a secret had been uncovered, but from that time on he no longer killed bears. His last time at the station he left his boat there together with the motor, and for it he got so many bullets and tobacco that clearly it would last him. Maksim didn't know how old he was, he never counted the years, but he felt that he'd been living a long time, longer than all those whom he remembered. He was becoming decrepit at a fast pace, his sight was getting worse, and he suffered from pain in his injured leg. He ate only birds that he managed to shoot right from his front steps. Occasionally his eyes would fail him and he thought that in the white haze covering his world, he saw large dark spots, the undefined shapes of bears.

Kolya Burkanov, a radio operator who had signed up for a year stint at the meteorological station, shot his first bear a kilometer and a half from the ruins of the former Selkup settlement. Kolya understood weapons and was not limited in means. His rifle had a telescopic sight and the clip was filled with explosive bullets, so that shooting from fifty meters he dropped the animal, having ripped open its throat. In a pleasant euphoria he walked up to the settlement buildings looking for a spot where he could dock a boat and bring out the pelt and the meat. On the steps of the only house still covered by a roof he found a dead man, who was looking nowhere with his white blind eyes. Kolya had heard something about this last inhabitant living his life out in this spot. He had a smoke, philosophically scratched his beard, looked for a shovel but could find nothing he could use. He dragged the body to a small hollow and covered it with branches, deciding to bury him properly when he returned with the boat.

But the same evening his coworker was medivaced out with an attack of appendicitis, and when they finally sent his replacement a week later, there was no reason to even think about the bear skin. He did remember the dead old man, but he shrugged his shoulders, having imagined what had become of his body. "Nothing left to bury there,–the replacement mumbled when he told him about that.–The bears have taken care of it." Kolya was only happy to agree with him.

ANSWER THE FOLLOWING

1. Did the Russification of local populations in the USSR have any positive result?
2. Was Maksim satisfied with his life?
3. What do we learn about the history of the Soviet Union from this story?
4. Are there any parallel events in the history of your country?
5. What can we do today to ensure that such events do not happen again?

DISCUSS THE FOLLOWING.

1. Does the author judge his country?
2. Was it justice to put Maksim in prison?
3. Does this story have any relation to your life and your future?
4. What makes this story specifically "Russian" and what makes it "universal"?
5. What is the role of the bear in this story?

COMMENTARY

HOPELESSNESS

By Mikhail Dymarsky

The best characterization of this story would be the formula "horrible in its simplicity." The narration is brief and neutral to the point of sterility, and yet it encompasses an entire century of human endeavor. It is the history of a state that had lasted as long as the century itself. An outsider who has never been to the Turkhan taiga can not possible tell how objective the narration really is. However, it is just too much like the truth, although reason and soul both just do not want to believe it. The story of Maksim and his nation is just too terrifying.

Mikhail Butov has actually described the history of the USSR using a few, probably key, moments, but he has described it from a most unexpected point of view for the Russian reader.[1] While any high school graduate today can easily explain *why* there was a campaign against illiteracy in post-revo-lutionary Russian society,*why* compulsory education was instituted, *why* and *for what reason* was there a war (the Great Patriotic War 1941–1945), *why* and *for what reason* did Stalin's terrifying repressions exist before the war and after it. While, I repeat, any school child today knows the answers to these questions, Butov's story brings these questions to a different level. *What was the reason* behind a campaign against literacy in the Selkup nation? *What was the reason* behind lifting the "strict ban" on the sale of *spirt* [alcohol]? Why were the Selkups supposed to provide fish for the front with which they were as familiar as with Kepler's laws? Why... Why... And finally what had they done to deserve it?

What had they done to have all this crash onto the innocent heads of this peaceful nation? They, the hunters and fishermen, strong and sure of themselves, but only in their own world. However, naive as children -disastrously naïve!-in all that the "new life" had brought them.

And actually, why did the Russians come to these lands? Why did they try to teach all the Selkups how to read and count and to give them an education? Why did they try to tame the unapproachable North, so rich in natural resources, but so severe? It is very simple: in order to build a new and happy world and to give them, the Selkups, a new and happy life. But to ensure this happiness by material means, the riches of the North had to be developed.

It is just that they forgot to ask the Selkups.

It would have been a good idea to ask. And if they could not ask the Selkups themselves (they did not speak Russian, you see), then they could at least have asked those people who knew this nation, their ethics, beliefs, traditions, way of life and value system. Maybe then they would have thought before destroying a way of life, albeit simple, but one that had taken centuries to form, before destroying traditions and beliefs so closely con-nected to natural conditions. In other words, to destroy a way of life which is *the only possible way of life* here in the barren and so severe Turukhan taiga. Here where the Selkups alone had lived from time immemorial, and where they are the only ones capable of surviving, because it took them centuries to adapt, because this is their native land, because the bear itself has always served not only as a source of meat and skin. It is not by chance that the author drops the phrase: "on the banks of the river from where his people had taken their genealogy." What underlies this phrase is an identification with nature so characteristic for pagan societies, an understanding of oneself not as a force counteracting nature, but to the contrary, as a part of nature itself. A certain detail is quite characteristic of this concept. No matter how much they taught Maksim in school, in his old age he behaves according to the stereotypes of his nation, particularly when he stops killing bears after the disappearance of his departed wife's body. And no wonder! What makes one wonder is how was it that those who came here without being asked did not understand that to try to change the Selkups into a part of the Soviet nation similar to the one they left behind is a vain undertaking. And that is in the best of cases.

And yet the Russian teacher accomplished much. She had taught them the Russian language, and she had managed to give them her faith in the "miracle," her faith in something fairytale-like and improbable, something that was supposed to happen at almost "any moment"... More terrifying, however, is the reality into which the waiting for the "miracle" had turned. Including even for the teacher herself. But herein lies the cruelty and horror of the power of statistics. No matter how horrible the suffering of an individual, no matter how bitter his untimely death, it appears that the suffering and disappointments of the Russian people do not carry as terrible, nor as fatal, historical consequences as the disappointments of the dying Selkups. With the death of the many, many millions of Russian people their culture, and their language have not been destroyed. With the death of EACH of the Selkups the inevitable disappearance from the face of the earth of this nation, its language, its culture, its beliefs, its hopes.... comes closer and closer.

What have you done? What have WE done? Out of an entire Selkup village there is one, and only one, man left, and there is no one even to bury him. The last "relic" disappears–and how can one correct all that has been done to these people? WHAT DID THEY NOT DESERVE, all in just a few decades, within one century of human endeavor?

THERE IS NO WAY.

SUCH MISTAKES ARE NOT CORRECTABLE.

(Particularly in today's Russia. If one thinks that the situation of the Far North nations has changed significantly in the current Russian state, one is gravely mistaken.)

Because this is not a mistake, but a CRIME. A chain of crimes carried out to a logical conclusion. They tried to make a people "happy", while using their land, their mastery of hunting, they used them as cheap labor, cynically paying in alcohol, and finally, not even trying to make them "happy" they simply forgot about them. Used and thrown out. And then they disappeared...

One can find a parallel with the murder of a person: the killer can be punished, but the punishment will not bring the victim back to life. And what about in this instance?

Painful? Yes.

Shameful? Yes.

Disappointing? Undoubtedly.

But what is most terrifying-HOPELESS.

DISCUSS THE FOLLOWING

1. Do you agree with Dymarsky's opinion that this story is simple?
2. Do you agree with Dymarsky's opinion that the narration of this story is "neutral to the point of sterility"?
3. What is the difference between a mistake and a crime, and how does this relate to this story?
4. What emotions does this story evoke for this critic? And for you?

IN THE THICK FOG,
TO SAY NOTHING OF ALL THE REST

INTRODUCTION TO THE STORY

As Katerina Clark, in her work *The Soviet Novel: History as Ritual*, states, "[T]he positive hero has always played a role in the great tradition of Russian literature."[1] Rufus Mathewson in *The Positive Hero in Russian Literature* explains that "Russian imaginative literature–perhaps more than any of the world's great literatures–has been concerned with the celebration of emblematic literary heroes."[2]. They were presented as heroes (larger than life) who were to serve as teachers to their audience. The *bogatyrs* (heroes in Russian folklore), although based on real people, were often portrayed as "types", larger than life heroes whose real exploits were lavishly embellished in the oral tales of early Russian culture. In addition, another form of medieval Russian literature the *vitae*, (*Lives of the Saints*, a collection of biographies arranged in a calendar form) presented "...stories about the life, sufferings or pious acts of people canonized by the Church, that is, officially recognized as saints whom it was permissible to worship."[3] The saints were presented as "heroes" whose lives were examples of Christian virtues. Both the stories of the *bogatyrs* and the saints followed a prescribed

---

[1] Katerina Clark, *The Soviet Novel: History as Ritual* (Chicago: University of Chicago Press, 1981), p. 46.
[2] Rufus W. Mathewson, *The Positive Hero in Russian Literature* (California: Stanford University Press, 1975), p. 13.
[3] Dmitry Likhachev (ed) *A History of Russian Literature 11th-17th Centuries* (Moscow: Raduga Publishers, 1989), p. 51.

formula, which included some realistic detail, but followed the literary conventions for each genre.

Mathewson explains that as the age of realism in the 19th century came to Russian literature, "...the requirements of realism reduced the hero's dimensions, and the writers' predominantly tragic view of experience muted the note of affirmation which had prevailed in the earlier, less sophisticated literary forms."[4] One can look at the heroes of Pushhkin's *Evgenij Onegin* (Onegin) and Lermontov's *A Hero of Our Time* (Pechorin) who are superfluous men, men who are dissatisfied with their lives, play on the emotions of others and look, unsuccessfully, for meaning in their lives. Some of the heroes of the nineteenth century literary works are men who are searching for, but never find, fulfillment (Turgenev's *Fathers and Sons*–Bazarov, Dostoevsky's *The Possessed*–Stavrogin, Tolstoy's *War and Peace*–Prince Andrei); they are alienated from others, and are certainly not presented as heroes whose lives are positive examples for an audience. They can be seen as "anti-heroes" or negative heroes. In contrast there are characters who attempt to "do good", at least philosophically, but in reality are still not presented as examples to be followed. (see Dostoevsky's *Crime and Punishment*–Raskolnikov, and *The Idiot*–Prince Myshkin)

In contrast is Nikolai Chernyshevsky's *What is to be Done?* which contains several heroes, whose lives are given as exemplary "types" to be followed. Mathewson explains, "Though the 'is' in his novel is hidden under a heavy gloss of 'should be,' he nevertheless insists on grounding his novel in the illusion of the contemporary and the everyday."[5] This type of hero is seen in the 20th century works of socialism realism, although the heroes of socialist realism are so typical, so stereotypical, that, as Katerina Clark explains, "His image is reminiscent not just of hagiography [religious literature of medieval Russia], which tells of a saint's religious virtue as illumined in his life, but also of those sections of the old chronicles that tell of the secular virtues of princes, of the feudal sense of honor, duty, valor, and service to one's country."[6] The writers of socialist realism believed (or were supposed to believe) that their works should inspire their audience, either by setting forth a pattern to be followed (in the form of the hero) or by transmitting the enthusiasm of the characters to the readers. These authors aimed to prove (or were expected to prove) that people themselves make history, and thus they presented their heroes as a part of the masses; upon reading such novels, the reader was expected to believe in his/her own ability to follow the exemplars. As a reader of one novel (*Time, Forward!*

---

[4] Rufus W. Mathewson, p. 14.
[5] *Ibid.*, p. 75.
[6] Katerina Clark, p. 47.

1932) exclaimed to the editor of a newspaper of the time, 18 August 1934, "I read the novel and so wanted to become like its heroes–these enthusiastic workers."[7]

The positive hero of socialist realism was limited in his/her life; there were definite limits and paths set down by the literary doctrine itself. As Krystyna Pomorska explains, "At the end of the thirties and the beginning of the forties, the positive hero reached the final crisis of his *raison d'etre*, because he turned out to be totally limited in his choices."[8] There is little free will involved in the hero's actions as these actions must be presented to the reader as examples which, when followed, would lead to the ideological remolding of the reader (according to the doctrine of socialist realism.) There is little choice, little free will, all is predictable.[9]

Now that socialist realism is no longer the artistic doctrine of Russia, and the communist regime has fallen, Russia and its literature have entered a new era where the old ideology is no longer relevant, and a new ideology has yet to be determined. This absence has emerged as there is no prevalent guiding force in society, and thus in literature. Alexandra George interviewed a teacher of Russian literature in the early nineties, and this educator explained what many are saying about contemporary Russian society, there is a lack of morality. "... when there isn't any ideology at all like today, it's far worse because a child cannot differentiate good from bad. Currently a child is inculcated with general values in school. That's not enough because upbringing at home is often deficient."[10] The question of "Where are we going?"[11] was central to the Soviet Union in the transitional period under Gorbachev's perestrojka and is still important today.

If there is no clear path to the future, no guiding principles for society, the heroes of literary works are no longer defined. What is a hero? What morality should a hero espouse? In Lavrishko's story "In the Thick Fog, To Say Nothing of All the Rest" the protagonist is an escaped convict, an unlikely hero who is aided by the pilot of the plane on which he escapes. This scenario is in opposition to that of socialist realist works of the Soviet Union; all who would help an escaped convict were considered to be guilty of rebuking authority, forbidden under the Soviet system. Lavrishko's story

---

[7] As quoted in T. Sidelnikova, *Valentin Kataev: ocherk zhizni i tvorchestva* (Moscow: Sovetskii pisatel', 1957), p. 112.

[8] Krystyna Pomorska (ed.) *Fifty Years of Russian Prose: From Pasternak to Solzhenitsyn* vol. 2 (Massachusetts: MIT Press, 1971), p. 6.

[9] *Ibid.*, p. 6.

[10] As quoted in Alexandra George, *Escape from "Ward Six": Russia Facing Past and Present* (Maryland: University Press of America, 1998), p. 59.

[11] Nancy Ries, *Russian Talk: Culture and Conversation during Perestroika* (Ithaca: Cornell University Press, 1997), p. 15.

presents the reader with many unanswered questions (questions which are being faced by Russians today): What makes a hero? What is authority? What moral standards are in effect? What is good? And what is bad?

VLADIMIR LAVRISHKO

ABOUT THE AUTHOR

Vladimir Lavrishko was born and raised in Kazan. He belongs to the 1960s generation. He has graduated from an institution of higher learning. His works have been published since the late1980s in Kazan, and from the early 1990s in Moscow journals (*October*). He writes not only short prose, but also poetry. Today he lives in Kazan.

IN THE THICK FOG,
TO SAY NOTHING OF ALL THE REST

By Vladimir Lavrishko

1990, KAZAN

Visibility was only forty meters. Where only a half hour ago you could see the top of a tree, now you could only hear the crows caw. One of the dark spots moved about, a crow made a deep semicircle toward Burov, flapped its wings a few times and again vanished into the fog.

Without taking his hands out of his pockets, Burov spit out the chewed Belomor cigarette,[12] straightened his jacket and returned to the hall. His patched-up bag guarded a place next to a man wearing glasses. The man kept on reading the paper. For the hundredth time, to be sure. His bag was on the armchair on Burov's side. Had he kept it on his lap, it probably would be in his way when turning the pages. And the floor was wet.

Burov picked up his bag, sat down and put it on his knees..

– Citizen[13]...

Burov's elbow twitched and bumped the bag, which fell directly onto the neighbor's newspaper.

– Do you have the time?

Burov inhaled and exhaled. Then he inhaled and exhaled again.

– Here... –he said after he exhaled the second time.

– What did you say?–said the man.

He probably thought that he just didn't hear.

–You, buddy,[14] behave as if you're in an office,–said Burov. Painfully official.

Must have gotten that from the papers.

---

[12] Belomor–a Russian produced brand of cigarettes, inexpensive, strong, generally smoked by common people.

[13] citizen–Russian *grazhdanin*, like the word "comrade" a common form of address after the Revolution. The communists tried to replace the seemingly genteel forms of Mister/Mrs./Miss and the use of a family title. "Citizen" was generally used for people whose names one did not know and sometimes implied a certain feeling of distance or disdain.

[14] man–Russian *muzhik*. Originally referred to a peasant. Currently can be a familiar form of address, or reference to a man, sometimes implying a certain amount of manliness and strength.

Burov twisted his wrist and looked at his watch. He wore the watch facing in. It was Lyubanya's[15] watch.

As of about ten hours ago he should have already been a corpse. Obviously they would have cut him up in his sleep. There'd be no autopsy today; it's Sunday. They'd have left him in the snow to keep him fresh.

–Twelve fifteen, said Burov.

... thieves all around and no one gives a damn,–said the man.

He pored over his newspaper for the hundred and first time. This time he read from the end.

–Hey, look. Boris Nikolaevich and Mikhail Sergeevich[16] are butting heads. Anatoli Ivanovich[17] is writing poetry.–The man hit the paper with the back of his hand.–Can you imagine? Nikolai Ivanovich is languishing in a hospital. Silaev[18] is giving a speech...

–And Pyotr Ivanovich[19] is attacking–said Burov.

Burov's fate was sealed. The zone[20] has its own hard laws, everyone for himself. But Burov couldn't just stand by and watch. There was nowhere to turn away to.

–Pyotr Ivanovich–the man asked.–Who's that?

Burov might have turned away. He had only a month and a half left to serve. But he could not simply stand by and watch. And he had a heavy hand.

–From the Supreme Soviet,[21] is he?

The thieves didn't touch Burov. They respected him. Well, respected

---

[15] Lyubanya's watch–Lyubanya is a woman whom the author has not discussed.

[16] Boris Nikolaevich–refers to Boris Nikolaevich Yeltsyn, who during the 1980s expressed a certain amount of opposition to Mikhail Gorbachev, but more so to traditional Communists.

Mikhail Sergeevich–refers to Mikhail Sergeevich Gorbachev who during the 1980s was the leader of the Soviet Union. During his tenure many debates and heated discussions in the Duma were aired on Soviet TV. He and Yeltsyn were often on opposing sides of these debates. The use of the first name and patronymic (the second name which means son of x–Nikolaevich, son of Nikolaj) is a formal form of address, but adds warmth and familiarity. A patronymic implies that morals and ethics were to be passed from the father to the son, not given by society by the government.

[17] Nikolai Ivanovich–Ryzhkov–refers to a past Prime Minister of the USSR.

[18] Silaev–Ivan Stepanovich–refers to Ryzhkov's successor (1990-1991).

[19] Pyotr Ivanovich–refers to Burov's fellow convict. At this point in the story Burov and the narrator are beginning to reconstruct what has happened to him during the last few days.

[20] zone–in this context, refers to a prison compound.

[21] Supreme Soviet–The highest organ of state power in the former Soviet Union. Legally the sole legislator. There were two chambers: the Council of the Union, whose numbers were based on the population (in 1958 there were 738 members); the Council of Nationalities (25 members for each of the 15 former republics, 11 members for each of the autonomous republics, 5 members for each of the autonomous oblast (administrative region), 1 member for each of the national okrug (administrative region.)

or not–he didn't get into any soul-searching conversations with them. In a word, they just didn't touch him. Simple men stuck together and criminals stuck together. If they put something under Burov's seat, he didn't pay attention, he just passed it on for smuggling out. He never got caught. He never asked anything from the criminals, spent no time in the infirmary. There was no place to carry on conversations about respect, no one to have them with, and no reason for them to be initiated. Once a certain trustee[22] needed CPR, and no one knew what to do, but Burov had learned how to do it in the army. Then he made a dash for the infirmary. The guy lived. Another time, right during inspection, he put his foot on a packet of some stuff. Someone in front had dropped it from his sleeve, and Burov stepped on it. If it's next to you, they'll interrogate you endlessly as well... And all that for soul-searching conversations.

After that one of their convicts approached him. A serious man. They chatted about nothing in particular–wife, children ... About the weather. Smoked in silence. And parted ways.

–From the Supreme Soviet, is he? Pyotr, you say? the man asked.

–Ivanovich? I do know...

Burov heard something.

–Cool it, buddy!–Burov raised his hand.–Quiet!

He thought he heard the sound of a motor. But the hall was noisy, and he couldn't hear properly.

Burov turned his head toward the exit onto the runway and sat still.

–And?

You could hear the engine noise again. You couldn't mistake it now.

–Is it coming? It's coming!–said the man.

He quickly grabbed his bag. He must have been a clever guy.

–Move it, or you're not gonna make it through–he threw the suggestion at Burov.

Burov twisted his way behind him into the crowd, but the door was already jammed with people. Burov's body was twisted sideways, and he was shoved out onto the runway. A small plane slithered out of the fog, and the noise was dying down. Skis dangled under the airplane fuselage. The airplane skidded above the runway, bumped the ground next to it, sat on the skis and plowed the snow toward the fencing. People were still pushing from behind, but the ones in the front had turned around and were already pushing back.

---

[22] trustee–prison term meaning a hardened, professional criminal, a common thief who lives exclusively under thieves' laws and subordinates himself only to a so-called "local thieves' authority person." In common speech it refers to a "cruel and stupid bandit."

There was a red cross on the plane.

Burov could not turn away. And the next day, in the garage, they told him to bust out tonight before roll call. The guy stood with his back to Burov, "doing his thing," and didn't once look at Burov. He was dressed in the same kind of pea jacket as Burov, except his was new. Under the pea jacket he was wearing gray overalls.

–If you want to live,–Burov recalled,–bust out before roll call. Bust out in a car–just keep going straight and don't stop.

Burov busted out right through the doors. He remembered the advice, they don't give advice there for nothing, and he pushed on. Bullets hit the body of the car, but all on the right side. In the cab there were three very precise bullet holes; he figured out later.–All on the right side.

They'll raid him. What they'll add to his sentence is of no import, he won't get a second chance. He has to run fast and far...

There was a red cross on the plane. The paint on the tail unit had bubbled up, and the bottom bubbles had peeled off. The fog was closing in behind the plane.–Medivac,–said the man.

Burov could see that for himself.

–Listen, who's this Pyotr Ivanovich?

–What Pyotr Ivanovich?–Burov couldn't understand.

He had to run farther away from here and was having trouble doing so. Fog, just to spite him.

The door of the pilot's cabin opened, and a young man in a short jacket with a worn out collar jumped out onto the snow.

–Hey, you man, what's with this Boris Nikolaevich, Nikolai Borisovich..[23]. What are they, your relatives?

–I'm interested in politics,–said the man–I'm concerned... Everything depends on them. Life and such... Does anything depend on us? And you with your Pyotr Ivanovich, Pyotr Ivanovich. What's his last name?

–Bagration,[24]–said Burov.

–A new one, is he?–said the man–From the Supreme Soviet?

The guy in the flight jacket walked across toward the building and turned into the heavy gray door. There was some kind of a tower on the top. All glass, almost. Flight controller's, probably.

–Yeah.–Burov's eyes followed the pilot until he disappeared behind the door.

[23] Nikolai Borisovich – note the use of the patronymic Borisovich, son of Boris, and its reversal of Boris Nikolaevich (Yeltsyn), son of Nikolai

[24] Bagration–1763-1812–a prince and general who was a famous hero of the Patriotic War of 1812.

–From the Soviet. From Fili.[25] A general, he is.

–Do you support the military?

A green van drove up to the plane. It also had a red cross painted on it. The driver and another guy in a white doctor's coat began to take a stretcher out of the back. Someone from inside the van was helping them.

–He's from the year eight hundred twelve,[26] buddy.–Burov watched as the guy in the white coat and tarpaulin boots almost tipped the stretcher over. Suffering from a hangover, probably.–He was even earlier, said Burov. –He'd already crossed the Alps.[27]

–The Alps!–The man switched the bag from one hand to the other. You're making fun of me... Is he a relative of yours?

– He's my uncle, said Burov.–The highest ideals inspire him; but when past joking he fell seriously ill, he screwed a Frenchman.[28]

The driver and the guy in a white coat carried the stretcher back to the plane. Someone covered up to his chin in a washed-out cotton flannel blanket was lying on the stretcher. The guy who almost dropped the stretcher walked behind them. His white coat was tied in the back with cloth tape. He hadn't seen such white coats, even in the zone.

–Let's go lie in the sun again,–said the man.–Now I don't even have anything to read. I left the paper, idiot...

A woman in a down filled scarf began to get out of the van. She was holding onto the door with her right hand and using her foot to find a place to step on.

Burov looked in his bag and got out a magazine. Back in the garage he had committed the address to memory, even though the guy only gave it to him once and didn't repeat it. Libknekht Street number 12. The bag, the clothes and the watch he was wearing came from there.

The woman found the ground with her foot and fell into the snow almost half way up her felt boot.

–There you go,–said Burov.

He had bought the only available magazine in the kiosk. The kiosk was still open in the morning.

–"Horse-Breeding",–the man read.–What's there to read here?

–What's the difference to you? Burov opened up the magazine.–All

---

[25] Fili–a Moscow suburb

[26] 812 refers to the War of 1812 between Napoleon and France when Napoleon invaded Russia, reached Moscow and was then pushed back to France.

[27] crossed the Alps-refers to General Aleksandr Vasilyevich Suvorov's legendary crossing of the Alps in the late 1700s.

[28] Frenchman–The highest ideals inspire him... –This is a quote from Pushkin's Eugene Onegin "... high ideals inspire him; but when past joking, he fell seriously ill." where Burov changes the end.

the horses and people blurred together...[29] There are pictures here.

He had studied the classics thoroughly. There had been lots of time. He got quite the education there. Only he didn't know—who had forced him into this early freedom with three bullet holes in the cabin?

—Good enough?—Burov asked.

—Good enough.—The man who had once had a cigarette with Burov was examining a swollen shiner.

The day before Burov had severely punished a couple of gummies.[30] Now they were demanding a meeting.

So, what have you got to say?

—You know the law.—One of the gummies was named Bubon,[31] and he turned his swollen black eye to the light, so everyone could see it.

I guess he's a harmless sucker,—said Chigrash.[32] Chigrash was the one on whom Burov had performed CPR, and whom he got to the infirmary in time. — Maybe he's just a psycho?

Outside they don't give a driver's license to a psycho out of jail. Even here they won't make a psycho a driver. The law is the law,—The law is the law,—said the gummy.

—As if you know anything! You motor mouth, you,—Chigrash said.

—Why are you shutting me up?—the gummy touched his black eye.

—Even outside they have glasnost[33]...

—Maybe you need a teleconference?[34]—The man who had had a smoke with Burov broke a pencil in his pocket.

—No need.—Gummy moved away just in case.

—He's gonna teach me about the law...—The man who had had a smoke with Burov was known to the authorities as Pyotr Ivanovich Krasnov, as Kostomarov, as Nagornyj, as Sanin, Ivan Petrovich.

—You yourself know the law.—This was said by another gummy.

---

[29] Lermontov's poem (1837) "Borodino" *Smeshalis v kuchu koni, ljudi,...* Horses and people mixed into a heap,..." The poem describes the battle of Borodino during Napoleon's invasion of Russia in 1812.

[30] gummies–prison slang meaning lackey (Russian *shestyorka* comes from the Russian word for six, the lowest card in the old style deck of cards.)

[31] Bubon–implies associations with the bubonic plague (black death) and the card suit diamonds; something round (fat, pudgy, plump) and fond of playing cards.

[32] Chigrash – a nickname derived from a first or second name of non-Russian origin (perhaps Tatar or Kirgiz.)

[33] glasnost–one of Gorbachev's slogan words referring to openness and the right to criticize and oppose; literally means " to have a voice". This was juxtaposed to the many years of silence and fear under his predecessors.

[34] teleconference–during the 80s a popular method of conducting meetings between two distant places. These orchestrated meetings aired criticism and differences of opinion while rallying support for Gorbachev's ideas. There were several of these between the USSR and the US.

–I know the law.

It was too bad about the pencil. The pencil was just a stub. To get a pencil was no problem, he was used to that. He dropped the broken pencil halves in his pocket and took his hand out.

–Deal, Chigrash.

He didn't even look at Chigrash. When Chigrash took out a deck of cards, he got up. And he took out a pack of Pamirs,[35] although he could have been smoking Marlboros.[36] If he had wanted to. But he was used to Pamirs. They weren't producing Pamirs anywhere these days,[37] but he always had a pack. He twisted the cigarette between his fingers and put it in the cigarette holder. Three lighters were immediately stretched out toward him. He got a light from a young man wearing a pea jacket, with a stylish pair of overalls. He, himself, was wearing a washed out plaid shirt.

He blew smoke out through his nostrils, nodded, and pointing with the cigarette holder to the young man he said:

–Woolly will make sure that everything is quiet. It's not a congress here. We'll get by without the press...[38]

–What don't you like about the press?–said Burov. There are pictures here. Here's a mare.–"Haberdashery"...

There was a picture of a mare.

–From the stud "Gallant" and the mare "Lottery"–read Burov.

The stretcher was lifted onto the plane. Both the driver and the guy in a white coat went back. The woman in the down scarf stayed by the metal stairs.

–OK, let's have it,–agreed the man.

The two with the stretcher returned to the car, pulled out some kind of box from it and carried it off to the plane. The guy in a white coat was walking pigeon-toed [clumsy]–apparently the box was not exactly light.

The pilot came out of the heavy, gray door, opening it with some effort,

---

[35] Pamir–Russian produced cigarettes, inexpensive. Famous sort of non-filtered cigarettes containing cheap and strong tobacco. A pack used to cost ten kopecks.

[36] Marlboro–the most commonly imported cigarette. Expensive and out of reach for the masses, but a symbol of status for those with connections.

[37] They weren't producing Pamir anywhere these days–During the 80s many items became not profitable to produce under the then new rules of self-financing, where a given enterprise was expected to stay in the black and not receive government subsidies. In the 1970s all cigarette factories produced Pamir cigarettes, but by the late 1980s only one or two factories in the entire USSR were still producing them. They were very inexpensive and therefore did not provide a profit to the enterprise.

[38] It's not a congress here. We'll get by without the press.–Under Gorbachev for the first time in many decades meetings of the legislative bodies were aired live on TV. This was a phenomenon for the viewing public, and the press was eagerly providing coverage of any and all meetings possible. The public was eagerly watching.

went down along the brick wall and now dove into the airport building through the regular entrance. Probably heading for the bathroom.

–Hey, buddy,–Burov handed the man his bag,–do me a favor. Take a look for a place for me there too. OK? I'll be right back.

The guy in a flight jacket was already coming out the door, pushing one of the glass panels.

–I'll just take a pee outside,–said Burov.

The man put the paper under his arm, grabbed the bag and went toward the building. The guy in the flight jacket caught up with him, got ahead of him and came out straight into Burov.

Burov stepped aside and already from behind caught up with him.

–Fellow townsman, be a friend,–said Burov.–Do this for me. That's the way it should be!

–What do you want?–The pilot stopped.–The plane is overloaded. Can't be done. And who are you, anyway?

Burov was standing almost next to the van.

The man in the white coat and the driver returned to the car.

–That's it! said the driver and raised his right hand. The man in the white coat already climbed into the cabin.

–Cheers!–said the pilot.

The driver slammed the door, lumps of snow flew out from under wheels and hit Burov.

–You a doctor, or what?–asked the pilot.

The van had made a turn at the runway fencing and began to disappear in the fog.

–A doctor,–said Burov.–A medic.

–Then that's another thing.–The pilot rocked on his feet.–A doctor I can take along. The patient is very sick, and we have to have a medic. I wasn't hired to transport corpses,–said the pilot.–Let's go...

The newspaper was lying on the seat. The seat was unoccupied. A lanky young man stretched out next to where Burov sat. His cap was pulled down over his eyes, and his eyes were closed. He stretched his legs way out in front of him. The man holding Burov's "Horse-breeding" shuffled in front of him and coughed into his fist. But the lanky one didn't even open his eyes.

–Citizen, this place is taken...

–I'm sleeping,–said the lanky young man,–don't bother me. And move aside, you're blocking my dreams.

He kept his eyes closed.

The man put the bag in the old place and sat down right on the newspaper. He put Burov's bag onto his lap.

–When he comes, you'll have to deal with him yourself,–said the man.

–These are his things. And this seat is his.

–Let me sleep, I'm warning you for the last time,–said the lanky one.

He moved his leg and opened an eye, the one closest to the man. Then he opened both eyes, looked at the man, looked at Burov's bag on his knees. Then he picked up the edge of his cap visor with his index finger.

–These are his things, you say?–said the guy.– And where is he loafing about?

–Went to the bathroom.–The man opened up his "Horse-Breeding" in the middle and began to flip through the rest of the pages.

–Seems I gotta go pee too.-The lanky guy got up.–If your buddy doesn't come, don't give the seat away to anybody.

Silently the man put Burov's bag on the now empty seat.

–OK now?–said the lanky guy in a short jacket with a zipper. There was a bulge on the left side of his jacket. He had no luggage.

–You guys can figure it out yourselves.

–We'll figure it out,–promised the lanky guy.

In the bathroom he opened the door of an empty stall, closed it and pulled on the second handle. There were only two stalls there. The second was locked. Behind the door someone was huffing and puffing, and under the door you could see someone pulling his pants up. The lanky one went up to the sink, turned the water on and waited for the door of the second stall to open. A man with a paunch came out holding a briefcase and went to wash his hands. The lanky one didn't wash his hands and went for the door.

–Where did you lose your buddy?–asked the lanky one.

–He's no buddy,–said the man.

He looked at the bulge in the jacket.

–Figure it out yourselves.–said the man.

He found an interesting article in the magazine, all about how they breed the mares and better the breed.

–He sat here, next to me, and then the medivac plane came...

–Medivac?–asked the lanky guy.

–Yah,–said the man.

–So, since he sat[39] here–then it's another story.–The lanky one looked around.

---

[39]   he sat–"to sit" also refers to sitting in jail when not followed by a place where one is sitting (i.e. chair)

–Then that's another story,–said the pilot.

They were walking toward the plane right through the unplowed snow, trying to step into the tracks left by the van driver and the medic. The pilot, wearing his flying boots and a jacket with a worn out collar, walked in front. He stopped and turned around.

–I'm taking you instead of the patient's wife. I can do it, since you're a doctor. She's not authorized. Let her take a scheduled flight...

The woman in the down scarf kept on waiting by the short metal steps next to the plane. Her face was swollen. She had either cried a lot or slept too little.

Burov stopped.

–No, chief, he said.–I won't take her place.

–Thank you, chief, he said.

–Medivac?–asked the lanky guy.

–Yeah,–said the man.

He finished reading about how they breed mares. There was nothing else of interest in the magazine. He lifted himself up off the seat, pulled out the newspaper from under it and smoothed it out on his lap.

–All right,–said the lanky guy.–Hold my place.

–Listen.–The man stopped him.–Do you know which Bagration they elected to the Supreme Soviet?

–Which Bagration?...–The guy was stepping over someone's luggage on the floor.

–Pyotr Ivanovich,–said the man.

–They did the right thing.–said the lanky guy while walking away. He had no time for chatting.

–No chief,–said Burov.–I won't take her place. Thanks. Go ahead, turn the propeller.

–The plane is overloaded. Now the pilot felt awkward in front of Burov.

He stomped in place, then kicked the ski.

–It's not going to take off,–he said.

–It's OK, chief,–said Burov.–You can wave your wings there to my people.

–You flying to see your wife?–asked the pilot.

–Yes.–Burov took out a pack of Belomor cigarettes and lit up.

–Haven't seen her in a long time?

–Quite a long time,–said Burov.

Once more the pilot kicked the ski with the tip of his flight boot.

–Get in,–he told the woman.

The woman went up the gangplank into the plane. The pilot detached it and threw it into the cabin. Then he kicked the ski once more.

–It won't take off,–he said to Burov.–They loaded it up with donors' blood...

–That's OK,–said Burov. Nothing to be done.

He turned and started walking toward the airport building. You could hear the crows cawing behind the building.

–Stop.–The pilot opened the door.–Get in. Maybe it will take off?

He was quickly making his way between the rows of seats. He stepped on someone's foot, then he got tangled in someone's bundles. When he opened the glass door of the gate, the noise of the airplane engine blew into the hall.

The lanky one ran out to the fence and froze.

The plane had already turned around, made it out onto the runway and twitching its wings was sliding into the milky white fog.

The lanky one opened his mouth, then he waved his hand; you could only hear the engine noise in the fog.

–Let's try.–said the pilot.–maybe we'll make it.

He bent across over Burov, opened and then shut the door on his side properly, and then pointed to the rope handle above the door, the kind of handle that they have in trams, to hold on to.

–Slam the door hard.–The pilot turned to the woman by the stretcher. Tie the handle with twine...

–Tighter,–he said.

–The bastard keeps opening,–the pilot said to Burov.

The pilot shoved the headset on his head. He moved the right one to the side; you could hear nothing in the headset.

–Here we go, with God!–The pilot winked at Burov.–We're off.

–Not a soul anywhere.–Burov twisted his neck and looked to the left and to the right.

–As it should be,–said the pilot.–But the overload should not be.

The pilot moved his hand down. The engine sneezed, roared, the propeller flashed and turned into a see-through foggy circle. Then the circle disappeared...

–Let's go.–The pilot took the second handle.

The plane twitched, lunged forward, turned around and rolled onto the runway, then turned around once more and began to gain speed.

Burov looked back. The field behind was empty, only some lanky guy was standing by the fence. The guy waved his hand and dissolved in the fog.

The pilot kept on looking at the quivering arrow on a black round dial. Then he moved the handle toward himself.

–Overload,–he said and then he let go of the handle.–We won't lift off.

The arrow on the black dial kept on dancing and moving up. The runway ended. The plane was speeding over the snow.

–Next stop–the ravine,–said the pilot.

Burov could see nothing but the fog ahead.

–We'll try,–said the pilot and pulled the lever again.

The plane lifted off the ground and hung in the fog. The tops of trees and the slope of the ravine flashed under Burov.

Burov looked at the altimeter. The arrow made it over a hundred meters and began to slowly inch its way up.

The pilot was making his first turn when, suddenly, something banged. The woman squealed and dug her nails into the back of Burov's seat.

–The damn thing opened,–said the pilot, without turning around.

–Listen, doctor.–The pilot finished his turn and leveled the plane.–Go and close the door, please. Tie the handle well with a piece of rope.

The air became noticeably fresher in the plane.

Burov lifted himself up, knelt on the seat, then crawled over the back of the seat and landed next to the stretcher.

The woman dug her nails into the back of the pilot's seat and no longer made any noises. The stretcher was attached to the posts. The blanket had slid off the patient and was fluttering, but from the patient himself, there was not a sound. He was probably really very ill. And he couldn't care less about anything.

The door moved back and forth when the plane hit air pockets and then was lifted up again. Through the doorway you could see solid white foggy milk.

–You gonna give me a parachute?–said Burov, making his way closer to the side. He was trying to hold on tight to some metal ribs there.–I don't know how to fly.

–Really?–For a second the pilot turned his attention away from flying and looked back.–It's not high from here. Catch the door by the string. Just hold on tightly.–said the pilot.

Burov put his hat on, tilting it to the side, and made his way to the opening. A gust of air hit him in the face. He clasped a bracket over the door even tighter with his left hand and tried to grab the swinging door by the string. He was getting nowhere. Then he grabbed the edge of the stretcher with his other hand, let go of the bracket, and with tiny steps moved toward the tail of the plane. Now he was on the other side of the door. There he also found a bracket. He grabbed it with his right hand. But even from here he could not reach the twine.

The pilot turned around and looked at Burov.

–Hold on,–said the pilot.

And he made a left turn. The door moved toward Burov.

Burov stretched his hand out, grabbed the twine and pulled the door toward himself. Then he tied it properly, and checked how it held without letting go of the bracket.

–That's it. Let's move on.–Burov made his way back, holding on to the edge of the stretcher.

The sick guy, it turned out, was really all white and blue. He was having trouble breathing.

–All's well, mother[40]–Burov said to the woman in a down scarf. – We're continuing our flight...

–So?–he said to the pilot and climbed back to his place over the back of the seat.

–We'll try,–said the pilot.

The pilot kept on looking forward, as if he could really see something. Burov couldn't even see the propeller. Noise and fog were the only things ahead.

–Fine weather!!!–shouted Burov.

The pilot pointed to the headset and shook his head. At first his right ear was a bit uncovered. Now he completely covered both of his ears with the headset. Burov had not noticed when he put them on like that.

–Can you get the pilot?–asked the lanky guy.

Before that, he had shown his red book[41] to everyone in the flight tower who needed to know.

Yes, we can,–said the guy at the control panel. He was sitting by the microphone with his shirt opened. It was warm inside.

–Get him then,–said the lanky guy.–Then give me the microphone.

–You don't have the authority.–said the radio operator.

–Raise him,–said the lanky guy.–Pass on what I say...

The radio operator clicked the switch, turned the tuning dial and muttered into the microphone:

–Ninety six, ninety six, come in, please, ninety six......

–Ninety six here,–said the pilot.

Burov looked at him. The pilot kept on flying into the fog.

–I've got him,–said the radio operator to the lanky guy.

–Tell him ...–said the lanky guy.

---

[40]   mother–an endearing form of address to a woman older than the speaker

[41]   red book–refers to the secret police ID book which was a "little red book" and was recognized and feared by soviet citizens.

The pilot kept on looking ahead and flying into the fog. Burov looked back; the woman was adjusting the patient's bed.

—I hear you.—said the pilot.

The radio operator clicked the dial and looked at the lanky guy.

—Now get me Srednevolzhsk,[42] —said the lanky guy.

—How far to Srednevolzhsk?—shouted Burov.

The engine was droning. And the pilot was wearing headphones.

—What's our flight time?—Burov shouted again.

He pulled up his sleeve and knocked on the dial.

—Forty minutes,—said the pilot.

They had already been flying for twenty minutes. Burov had checked the time when they took off. He hadn't had time to pee, and now his bladder was bursting. But he could last another twenty minutes.

The woman in the back was making noises again, squealing something. The engine noise was making it impossible to understand. Burov turned around.

—What do you want mother?

—Doctor, doctor!—her scarf had fallen back off her head, her hair was disheveled.—Do something! Give him a shot.... he's in bad shape!

The pilot was wearing his headset. He was looking into the fog. What did he see in that fog?

—I'm coming,—said Burov.

He made it over the back of the seat and crouched down next to the stretcher. He took the patient's hand. The hand was cold and clammy. He took the wrist where doctors check for the pulse. Only he forgot from which side. There didn't seem to be anything there. Burov took the hand the other way, squeezed the fingers, moved them both ways. Under his fingers he could feel something weakly slipping away with interruptions.

—I'm dying...—suddenly the man on the stretcher said.

His nose became even more angular.

Nothing doing!—said Burov,—You're gonna live whether you want to or not. Everything is fine papasha..[43] The heart beats, the nose twitches.[44] Stop this silly thinking.

—Give him some kind of a shot.—said the woman.

—I have no syringes with me,—said Burov.—Only don't panic. He's dying... It only seems that way. It seems death is right around the corner,

---

[42] Srednevolzhsk–a fictional town name. It seems to refer to a real town due to its resemblance to Verkhnevolzisk.

[43] papasha–an endearing form of papa (father) used when the speaker is younger than the man addressed.

[44] the heart beats, the nose twitches–as long as the nose twitches, you are still alive (a Russian proverb)

that's it!–and again you're among the living. You gotta live, you will live. We'll make it without the syringes. I studied with Kashpirovsky[45] himself. We'll get by without....

The woman opened her mouth and looked at Burov with wide opened eyes. She hadn't fixed her scarf yet.

–I'm giving directives[46]–said Burov.–It'll be easier to breathe. Heartbeat is good, moving the blood to all the right places.

–I'm giving directives for breathing,–said Burov.

–I'm influencing the bio-field.

He put his hand on the patient's forehead. His forehead was damp.

The pilot again looked at Burov and then turned around.

–You will live, without a doubt,– said Burov.–I'm giving such a directive. Breathe, breathe... Everything will stabilize in a minute.

Under Burov's hand the forehead really did seem to dry. The man also stopped twitching and began to breathe more evenly.

Burov sat with him for another five minutes.

–See,–he said.–And you were planning on dying. We're gonna live.

Burov made it back to his seat. His bladder was about to burst, especially when he was climbing over the seat. Burov looked at the watch. They had already been in the air for forty five minutes.

–Chief!–yelled Burov.

The pilot moved one earphone aside.

–Are we landing soon?–said Burov.

The pilot shrugged his shoulders.

–Listen, I'm gonna pee out the door, OK?

Burov grabbed the handle. The pilot shook his fist at him.

Then he opened up the map case, and pulled out a map. He started to examine it on his knees. Then he looked down.

–Tokushkino,[47]–he said.

He pointed down for Burov. Burov stared down; some little village was barely visible floating between breaks in the fog. But Tokushkino was completely on the other side of Srednevolzhsk. Means the fly boy got lost. From Tokushkino it was still another twenty minutes.

---

[45] Kashpirovsky, Anatolij Mikhailovich – a healer who claims to be able to operate on people without the use of anesthetic. During the 80s a very popular individual, often shown on TV, written about in papers and magazines.

[46] I'm influencing the bio-field. I'm giving directives - to influence by using the biofield. It is meant that the source of the field is the man who says it, his unseen energy. Burov imitates Kashpirovsky and others like him who claimed to influence others to act just by a concentrated look or passing one's hands over another.

[47] Tokushkino–a city, probably made up by the author

Burov nodded to the pilot to show him he understood.

–What's with him?–The pilot indicated back with a nod of his head.

–He's alive,–Burov said.–He'll live. This is almost a Poperessus Propulsion.[48]

–It happens,–said the pilot.

–But, that's a long story.–said Burov.

The pilot nodded, put on his headset again. He flew on, from time to time peeking at the map.

–So, that's that,–said the man whom they called the trustee in the zone and others called Pyotr Ivanovich Krasnov. Actually he was the King. He was rolling the broken stub of a pencil in the pocket of his pea jacket. Somehow he had managed to sharpen it again.–So this is the way it stands...

There was a lot of trouble in the zone after the break out. They barely managed to get the meeting together. He looked at the gummy, whose shiner had become less colorful and somewhat yellowed. The gummy, whose nickname was Bubon, pushed back deeper into the shadows.

But the King's glance didn't even look his way. He let go of the pencil.

–I can't see it. Where's his spot?–he said.

His spot's by the john,–answered Chigrash. Chigrash sat, resting his hands on his knees.

–We're not gonna vote?–The trustee lifted up the tip of his lip and then let it drop. That for him was a smile. He got up. He went down the passageway. Then he turned around.

–Woolly will take care of it,–he said.–If ... we're gonna punish him.

–That's the law,–he said.

He opened the door of the barracks and walked out into the fog. But in the twenty years he spent here he'd learned to go around even blindfolded.

Burov couldn't see a damned thing in this fog. But the plane began its descent. In a minute the skis were already sliding along the snow. But, for some reason, you couldn't see any buildings there. On the right stretched a wooded strip. Only in the far distance could you see a flicker of the airport building.

–I missed it...-said the pilot.–Fog... But, if you need a trolley, it's closer from here.

–Thanks.–Burov grabbed the door handle.–What's your name? Maybe

---

[48] Poperessus Propulsion–a fabricated nonsense expression derived from "puls" (*puls*-pulse) and "poperechnyj" (*poperechny*-transworld) with a Latin ending. The fabrication is based on the sound of its syllables.

we'll meet again. Pig won't bump into a pig, but a man can always meet a man again,–said Burov.

–Pyotr Ivanovich,-said the pilot.

He was rolling his map and putting it back in the case.

–Look!–Burov said. We're namesakes...

He had a passport in his pocket, one they gave him on 12 Libknenekht Street. In it he was listed as Pyotr Ivanovich.[49]

Burov turned toward the stretcher.

–I'm giving the directive to live!–said Burov.

He opened the door, jumped into the snow. Right behind the first tree he relieved himself. He walked off toward the trolleybus stop.

The plane turned around, spraying a cloud of snow. He rolled off toward the airport. The runway was now deserted. Already on the approach way he was stopped by a police van. First a policeman in a captain's uniform jumped out, then two guys in civilian clothes. The civilians ran to the side, where Burov had just been sitting, and the captain walked up closer to the pilot.

–Where?—asked the captain.

He had already looked into the cabin.

–He jumped out, left...–said the pilot.

The pilot looked back. The patient was lying there quietly. The door was tightly tied with a white strip of cloth. It would probably take a long time to untie it.

–I'll let you rot in jail,–promised the captain.–Look where you landed.

The pilot shrugged his shoulders.

–Fog...–he said.

The captain's radio crackled in his chest pocket. The captain took it out and put it to his ear, then he pushed a button.

–No, Pyotr Ivanovich,[50]–the captain said,–he left...

Then he pressed the button again. Again he listened. He listened for a long time. It appeared that they were really chewing him out. The two in civilian clothes came up to the captain and stood next to him.

–Well, Ivan Petrovich?[51]–asked one of them.

Instead of answering, the captain again pressed the button.

–Fog...–the captain said into the radio.

This story was already familiar to him. So, he broke out. Driver. He

---

[49]   Pyotr, son of Ivan (Ivanovich)

[50]   The person he is speaking to has the same name as the pilot and Burov's new name (which is on his fake passport.)

[51]   Note the reverse of the previous name: Ivan son of Pyotr (Petrovich)

almost finished his term. He punished two gummies and took off in a car.
The captain would have done so as well. Let those who have nothing to do
try and catch him. There are so many to catch here you don't have time.
Where was he supposed to look for him now? They didn't have any dogs.
He's not a dog himself. And snow up to the knees. In this fog the devil
could break a leg.

    –Consider it done,–said the captain into his radio.–Got it.

    –Fog, Pyotr Ivanovich, fog...–said the captain.

    He turned the radio off. Adjusted it on his chest.

    – ...If you don't take anything else into account...

    He mumbled this under his breath.

ANSWER THE FOLLOWING

1. What do you know about Gorbachev, his policies, the country under him?
2. Does the life of prisoners, as discussed by Lavrishko in this story, differ from the life of prisoners in your country?
3. Who are the positive heroes and who are negative?
4. Do you agree with what the pilot did?
5. Why did the patient feel better after Burov's help on the plane? What do you think about this kind of treatment? Why might it have been so popular in the Gorbachev and Yeltstyn period of the Soviet Union and Russia?

DISCUSS THE FOLLOWING

1. Why did the author choose this title?
2. Is there any optimism in this story?
3. What do you think would happen if the plot of the story were to continue?
4. What is the role of the man sitting next to Burov?
5. Why do so many of the characters have similar or the same names? What does the author want to show?
6. What unique aspects of Soviet-Russian society and culture are presented in this story?

COMMENTARY

TO STOP A MOMENT, TO EXTEND HOPE...

By Mikhail Dymarsky

One of the merits of this story is the fact that it is open-ended. That is because one does not want to ponder "what will happen next". One does not have to be a psychic to predict the immediate future awaiting Burov. Captain Ivan Petrovich refuses to chase the escapee in knee-deep snow, in a fog in which the devil could "break a leg." In a way he lets Burov go knowing his "history," but the captain, although he knows life and himself is just tired, is not the entire police force. "Let those who have nothing to do try and catch him" – Captain Ivan Petrovich thinks morosely. And he does know that there will be those who will try. And then Burov will get another sentence, he will get the maximum for escaping; there is no doubt in that. And, in addition, it is quite possible that he will be returned to the same penal colony, and that there he will be met by the same prisoners "with connections", the very same ones who "sentenced" him and from whom he was running...

And if, perchance, Burov manages to hide somewhere where he won't be found, "only where?", and will he have to hide for the rest of his life? Live under an assumed name, always afraid that he will be found, recognized? Not a very positive outlook for the future... And the criminal elements–they will search for him, and they will find him, maybe even faster, for they have long arms, longer than the arm of the police. It is enough to look at the "lanky young man" with the "red book," apparently a policeman's ID, where the only thing that remains unknown–is the book real or is it a forgery? He bears little resemblance to a policeman–his behavior, his speech, his body language and his looks. On the other hand he bears a close resemblance to a criminal who pretends to be a "cop"...

So, it is a good thing that the story ends where it ends.

Although, in truth, the story is not about that, not about Burov's successful escape and how justice prevailed. What justice can there be among the savage laws of the "zone," those which follow Burov even on the outside!

The *sjuzhet* of this story is composed of a chain of fantastic lucky chances. In the beginning Burov, who has been "sentenced" to death is warned about the danger and is advised to run. And who does this? The King's right hand, the one they call "Woolly." Then, during the most awful, hopelessly stormy weather, a small medivac plane arrives and the pilot, having heard the word "doctor" which Burov had thought up just in time, takes him on board, even though the plane is overloaded. The plane manages to take off.

But the most surprising is still ahead. The pilot is told on the plane radio that there is an escaped convict on board, and they warn him that the plane will be met on the runway in Srednevolzhsk by special forces. And what does the pilot do? He pulls a fast one and flies up to the city from the other side, lands the plane far from the airport and lets the "doctor" out. Did he do this on purpose or did he really lose his bearings in the fog–who knows? Fog...

But there is still that "everything else." What everything else?

Nothing is left to chance in this story. Burov is warned and told to run not "just like that," but remembering that he had more than once saved "the connected ones," saved without consideration if this was one of his people or not, and without asking for favors in return. The King is the Trustee, he is Pyotr Ivanovich and, as such he cannot go against the the thieves' "laws", or he will lose his authority. However, the King's unwitting respect for Burov makes him give Burov a chance: of course it was he who ordered the "Woolly" one to warn Burov.

The pilot, Pyotr Ivanovich, breaking all rules, takes Burov on board, feeling respect for this man when he "so needed" the place, which was his as a doctor almost by law, and which he gives up to the wife of the patient. And the pilot, having found out whom he has on board, helps him disappear because right in front of his eyes Burov had "healed" the dying patient no worse than any other doctor, but for no reward, just with human compassion and a willingness to help. And this, in Pyotr Ivanovich's eyes, is probably more important than all the verdicts, judgments and escapes. There are many ways a man can land in prison: anyone can stumble. Fog …

And the captain, Ivan Petrovich, had seen many such stories in his time. You did not have to explain to him that a man who had spent his time behind bars without any trouble does not escape a month and a half before the end of his sentence. That means there had to have been extraordinary circumstances; as a matter of fact his reasons had to have been very serious if he had "beaten up two gummies"–and the connected ones do not forgive. "The captain would have done that himself."

The coincidence of names is also interesting. Everyone who has a part in Burov's being saved has a name like his: either Pyotr Ivanovich or Ivan Petrovich.[1] The author underscores a certain spiritual connection, which joins these very different people: the driver, the thief, the medivac pilot, the police captain. All is very simple: in the most varied social strata, in the most varied situations there are those values that are most dear. These are unselfishness and justice, including the inability to tolerate injustice. They lead and save people while everything around drowns in total fog–just as the nameless man in glasses, who is rather unpleasant and who is consumed by politics of which he has no understanding, disappears....

One really wants the story not to continue. It is precisely now, when justice prevails, albeit temporarily, a hope is born that the Pyotr Ivanovichs together with the Ivan Petrovichs will find a way that leads out of the fog.

As improbable as that may be, such is the nature of hope.

DISCUSS THE FOLLOWING

1. Do you agree with Dymarsky's opinion that it is appropriate that this story ends when it does?
2. What coincidences are there in this story? What role do they play?
3. Why does this story begin and end in the fog? What could the fog symbolize?
4. In this story are there hints of the political situation in the country during this time?
5. Is there the promise of hope in this story?

SUGGESTED BIBLIOGRAPHY

GENERAL BIBLIOGRAPHY

Brown, Deming. *Soviet Russian Literature since Stalin*. New York: Cambridge University Press, 1978.

Brown, E. J. *Russian Literature since the Revolution*, New York: Collier Books, 1969.

Mathewson, Rufus. *The Positive Hero in Russian Literature*. 2nd ed. California: Stanford University Press, 1975.

Slonim, M. *Soviet Russian Literature: Writers and Problems 1917-1977*. 2nd ed. New York: Oxford University Press, 1977.

Struve, Gleb. *Russian Literature under Lenin and Stalin, 1917-53* Norman: University of Oklahoma Press, 1977.

DISCUSSION OF SOCIALIST REALISM

Clark, Katerina. *The Soviet Novel: History as Ritual*. Chicago: University of Chicago Press, 1981.

Ermolaev, H. *Soviet Literary Theories, 1917-1934. The Genesis of Socialist Realism*. New York: Octagon Books, 1977.

Hoskings, Geoffry. *Beyond Socialist Realism*. New York: Holmes and Meier, 1980.

Parkhomenko, Mikhail and Miasnikov, Aleksandr (ed.) *Socialist Realism in Literature and in Art*. transl. C. V. James. Moscow: Progres Publishers, 1971.

Tertz, Abram. *On Socialist Realism*. New York: Pantheon Books, 1960.

Vaughan, J. C. *Soviet Socialist Realism: Origins and Theory*. New York: St. Martin's Press, 1973.

WESTERN DISCUSSION OF RUSSIAN LITERATURE

Goscilo, Helena and Lindsey, Byron (ed.) *Glasnost: An Anthology of Russian Literature under Gorbachev.* Ann Arbor, Michigan: Ardis Press, 1990 (see introduction)

Marsh, Rosalind. *History and Literature in Contemporary Russia.* New York: New York University Press, 1995.

Shneidman, N.N. *Soviet Literature in the 1980s: Decade of Transition.* Buffalo: University of Toronto Press,1989.

Russian Literature 1988-1994: The End of an Era. Buffalo: University of Toronto Press, 1995.

Thompson, Eva M. (ed.) *The Search for Self-Definition in Russian Literature.* Texas: Rice University, 1991.

SUGGESTED STORIES AND FILMS

There are many more stories that would be of interest to readers of contemporary Russian fiction, and these are just a sampling of works dealing with topics similar to those included in this book. We suggest that those interested also look for other writings of the authors below as many of these writers have published many other works (stories, poetry, plays, novels) which have been translated into English.

A ROMANCE WITH A SEQUEL

Women's themes and/or male/female relationships

STORIES

Anton Chekhov, "Lady with a Lapdog" (1899)

Anna and Gurov, both married, meet at a resort on the Black Sea. Gurov, expecting an affair, realizes upon his return home that he cannot stop thinking of Anna. Chekhov portrays the agony of their feelings for one another while at the resort (without their spouses) and as they meet back in Moscow.

Natalia Baranskaya, "A Week Like Any Other" (1969)

Baranskaya tells the story of a "typical" Soviet woman who works as a technical research assistant at a scientific institute and has a husband and two children. This objective account of one week in her life provides insight into Soviet society and the three jobs Olga holds: her work, her family and her home.

Lyudmila Petrushevskaya, "Nets and Traps" (1974)

The narrator recalls her life at the age of 20 when she is pregnant and travels to her "husband's" mother in another city in order to have her child. She expects that Georgii will follow, legalize their marriage (he is still married to another woman who lives with his child in the same town as his mother) and begin a life together. Her situation is a result of circumstances, not nets and traps deliberately set.

Tatiana Tolstaya, "Dear Shura" (1985)

Aleksandra Ernestovna is an old woman who is alone, living with her memories. She reminisces about her youth when she was beautiful, and her life was gay;however, she did not join her true love (she was married at the time and he was poor, with nothing.)

Maria Arbatova, "My Teachers" (1995)

This autobiographical story tells of the author's teachers in school and institute and her teachers in life (doctors who attempt to correct her lameness) and her lovers and husbands. She describes her search for a true teacher, like her first teacher in school.

I. Grekova "No Smiles" (1970)

A woman scientist admits that she no longer follows the rules of the game. As a result, there is to be a commission to investigate her "fallacious orientation in research." She is no longer considered a "success", and she loses not only her prestige at the institute, but also her second laboratory room and the smiles of those with whom she works. At the end of the story "truth wins out" and once again she is met with smiles.

FILMS

Little Vera (1988)

Moscow Doesn't Believe in Tears (1979)

RELIC

Works whose action takes place in rural Russia/Soviet Union and deal with "old ways", customs and traditions. Films: non-urban Soviet Union/Russia, civilization meets traditional ways.

STORIES

I. Turgenev, "Bezhin Meadow" (18??)

In this story the author balances descriptions and narrative about nature when he tells the tale of a hunter who spends the night with some peasant boys. The stories told by the boys portray the rich peasant culture of that time.

Fyodor Abramov, "Wooden Horses" (1969)

This first person narrative is told in the voice of a visitor to a rural village who is looking for quiet and a place to hunt, fish and collect berries and mushrooms. He tells the story of a visit from his host's mother, a strong woman who works tirelessly collecting mushrooms and helping others. Stories from her life tell of her struggle to survive the backward ways of her husband, his family and the village.

Valentin Rasputin, "Downstream" (1972)

Viktor, after 5 years away, takes a journey on the river to return to his native village and muses about important memories of growing up on the banks of the river. The river has been flooded in order to produce a reservoir for a hydroelectric station, and many villages and lives have been destroyed since the government relocated them.

Anatoly Genatulin, "Rough Weather" (1987)

This story takes place on a collective farm in Bashkiria (a constituent republic of eastern central Russia). A five-year-old child becomes lost in the woods, and the circumstances of her disappearance (neglect and alcoholism of her father) as well as those of the search for her (lack of resources and, at times, true caring) lead to a tragic end. Genatulin portrays the inefficiencies of Soviet society, as well as the backwardness of those who live in this rural region.

Fazil Iskander, "Old Hasan's Pipe" (1987)

Hasan, an old shepherd, tells the narrator stories which paint a picture of village life in Abkhazia (a republic located between the eastern shores of the Black Sea and the edge of the main Caucasus mountains.) The beauty of nature is contrasted with the negative influences of Soviet/Russian society, such as alcoholism, *pokazukha* "appearances are everything."

FILMS

Dersu Uzala (1975)

Urga (Close to Eden) 1991

A STRANGE EVENT

Works of science fiction and fantasy

STORIES

Nikolai Gogol, "The Nose" (1836)

Collegiate Assessor Kovalev awakes one morning to find that his nose has disappeared. The nose subsequently appears as an officer whose rank is above that of Kovalev. At the end of the story, when Kovalev finds his nose has returned (perhaps with a pimple), Gogol suggests that perhaps the whole story was a dream. Or was it?

Vladimir Grigoriev "Vanya" (1960s)

Vanya is an exceptional child, a genius who, at the age of four, is able to comprehend higher mathematics. In the basement he builds a time machine, still imperfect, which can transport the narrator (Vanya's friend) and Vanya back in time. When his parents quarrel, Vanya sets the machine to turn back time to before the quarrel. However, the machine malfunctions, and it is years earlier. Vanya cannot return from the past, and his parents (who have yet to meet) walk away from one another and never meet.

Arkady and Boris Strugatsky, "Six Matches" (1960)

Scientists in the society presented in this story are so dedicated to the advancement of science that they perform dangerous experiments (research in neutrino acupuncture) using themselves as subjects. The authorities disapprove of this practice.

Valery Popov, "Dreams from the Top Berth" (1987)

A trip on a train becomes a ride of absurdities. The narrator, who has obtained his ticket *na levo* (from the left), believes he cannot complain about the problems he encounters since he did not pay for the ticket. The conductor is keeping chickens in the bathroom, the restaurant has only goulash (meat stew) from which the waiters have allegedly stolen the meat.

Andrei Bitov, "Pushkin's Photograph (1799-2099)" (1987)

This science fiction tale takes place in the past, present and future as the hero (a literary scholar) is sent into the past in a time machine, and meets Pushkin. He cannot relate to Pushkin as a fellow writer, and becomes a character similar to Pushkin's character Eugene in "The Bronze Horseman."

Viktor Pelevin, "Vera Pavlovna's Ninth Dream" (1994)

Vera Pavlovna works as a public attendant in the men's toilet. When Perestroika comes to the Soviet Union, changes occur in the public toilet: toilet paper is available, new tiles are installed, and there is music in the toilets. Vera questions this mystery of life. Manyasha, the attendant in the women's toilet, whispers this answer to her. This public toilet (which later is refurbished into a commission shop where Vera notices what seems to be excrement on the customers, and her dead brother begins to work at the shop) becomes the threshold into an alternate reality.

FILMS

Ivan Vasilevich: Back to the Future (1973)

Stalker (1979)

IN THE THICK FOG, TO SAY NOTHING OF ALL THE REST

Works of morality

STORIES

Fyodor Dostoevsky, "The Grand Inquisitor" (1879)

In this section of the novel Brothers Karamazov the Inquisitor believes that human beings will give up their freedom to choose in exchange for bread. Dostoevsky explores the question of free will and choice.

Ivan Bunin, "The Gentleman from San Francisco" (1915)

An American businessman dies while in Europe, and he is shipped back home. Bunin examines the modern day problem of indifference to the outside world, a preoccupation with oneself. The place where the businessman dies, Capri, is beautiful. As two peasants visit the statue of Madonna (on Capri), their simplicity and affinity to nature is contrasted to the materialistic world of the dead businessman.

Vasily Shukshin, "Snowball Berry Red" (1973)

This story, written as an outline for a film (later directed and starred in by Shukshin himself) tells of Egor, recently released from prison, who is trying to reform his life. He travels to a village to visit a woman (a typical unspoiled Russian village girl) with whom he has been corresponding. He tries to create a new life for himself based not on crime (as was his former life), but on old traditional values.

FILMS

Snowball Berry Red (1974)

Brother (1997)

A DEFROCKED MONK
Works of religious nature

STORIES

Lev Tolstoy, "What Men Live By" (1881)

Mikhail has been sent back to earth by God as a punishment since he had disobeyed God. He is sent to learn three truths: What dwells within man; what is not given to man; what men live by. Mikhail, through his experiences, learns that Love lives within man, man does not know his own needs and thus should live with others, and men live by love which, according to Tolstoy, is in God.

Babel, "The Odessa Stories", "The Red Cavalry" (two series of stories 1921-1930s)

This series of stories reveals Babel's fascination with Jewish characters. The Jewish figures of "The Odessa Stories" are surprising and unconventional: the Jewish gangster, Benya the King; Yid-and-a-Half, a millionaire; Manka, a matriarch of Jewish bandits. In "The Red Cavalry" Babel describes the military campaign of the Soviet Red Army into the region of western Ukraine and eastern Poland. The Jewish fighters of these stories have been transformed from inhabitants of isolated Jewish shtetls to warriors fighting alongside the fierce Cossack fighters.

Panteleymon Romanov "A Mistake" (1922)

The Komosols (Young Communists) plan their own Easter celebration (since under socialism, religion has been banned.) They face all the problems under early socialism, shortages, uneducated youth, miscommunication from the ministries. Romanov ironically refers to the change in the calendar (from the Gregorian to Julian) when the Easter service has been moved from midnight (the traditional beginning of the Easter service) to 2 AM.

Yury Kazakov "Goblins" (1960)

While walking home from an unsuccessful visit with a former teacher, Zhukov meets Matvey, the night watchman, who tells Zhukov about the Goblins in the field. Zhukov does not believe him and begins walking home as it turns dark. He hears wailing and sees shadows, but he convinces himself that these are just trees and forest animals. This story examines the question of the supernatural, superstition and perceived reality and by extension their possible implications for religious beliefs.

FILMS

Andrei Rublev (1966)

Commissar (1967)

Arna Bronstein

I was born in New Jersey and lived there until I left for college. In choosing a profession, I looked back a generation to my grandparents, who emigrated from Russia and Poland in the late 1890s and early 1900s, and chose Russian. I received my BA in Russian Studies from Colgate University, and my MA and PhD in Slavic Literature from the University of Pennsylvania. I began teaching at the University of New Hampshire in 1981, shortly after the Russian major was developed. My teaching interests focus on language teaching (all levels) and contemporary Russian society, especially women and family issues.

Aleksandra (Aleksa) Fleszar

I was born in Poland, where I lived for the first 14 years of my life. I received my BA from SUNY Buffalo and my MA and PhD from Ohio State University. Although my PhD was in Slavic Literatures, my training included Slavic Historical Linguistics and Culture and Civilization. I began teaching in 1976 at the University of New Hampshire, where by 1981 I developed the Russian major and a national study-abroad program. My current interests range from language pedagogy to film and contemporary Russian cultural studies, including contemporary society.